D0193402

MONEY
without
MADNESS

MONEY

without

MADNESS

Organize Your
Budget and Stop Money Stress
on Any Income

Karen Brigham, CPA, MBA

Adams Media Corporation
HOLBROOK, MASSACHUSETTS

Copyright ©1993, 1998, Karen Brigham. All rights reserved.
This book, or parts thereof, may not be reproduced in any form
without permission from the publisher; exceptions are made
for brief excerpts used in published reviews.

Published by
Adams Media Corporation
260 Center Street
Holbrook, MA 02343

ISBN: 1-58062-050-7

Printed in the United States of America
J I H G F E D C B A

Library of Congress Cataloging-in-Publication Data
Brigham, Karen.
Money without madness : organize your budget and
stop money stress on any income / Karen Brigham.
p.   cm.
Includes index.
ISBN 1-58062-050-7
1. Finance, Personal. 2. Cash flow. 3. Saving and investment. I. Title.
HG179.B7276   1998
332.024—dc21   98-33531
CIP

This publication is designed to provide accurate and authoritative information with
regard to the subject matter covered. It is sold with the understanding that the publisher is not engaged in rendering legal, accounting, or other professional advice. If
legal advice or other expert assistance is required, the services of a competent professional person should be sought.
     — From a *Declaration of Principles* jointly adopted by a Committee of the
American Bar Association and a Committee of Publishers and Associations

This book is available at quantity discounts for bulk purchases.
For information, call 1-800-872-5627 (in Massachusetts, 781-767-8100).

Visit our home page at http://www.adamsmedia.com

For my mother, Patricia, who taught me
    the beauty of art and the joy of creativity.
And for my father, John, who taught me
    the rewards of work and the value of money.

Table of Contents

Preface

Several years ago I wondered why I rarely knew how much money I had to spend and why I was unable to save any of it. As the controller of a successful company I knew all the financial details of a multimillion-dollar business. Why was my own purse a mystery to me? The guesswork and uncertainty motivated me into action, and I decided a budget would cure all.

A budget—no problem, I thought. I'm a CPA, an MBA, a financial professional—this will be easy. But when I tackled the project, I encountered complexities I didn't expect: Many of my expenses came monthly and didn't coincide with my biweekly paychecks. There was no way I wanted to track the small amounts of money I spent on food, entertainment, gas, and drugstore purchases, only to find the total exceeded my initial guess and my budget had failed. What about surprise expenses that always turned up and items I wanted to buy that I hadn't anticipated? Most importantly, I didn't want to work with my budget all month long. I wanted to do it *once* at the beginning of each month and let the system work *automatically* after that. It was soon clear a traditional budget didn't help at all. I wanted a simple system that guaranteed results.

THE MONEY WITHOUT MADNESS SYSTEM

Over the next couple of years I developed the *Money Without Madness System* presented in this book. Using this system I saw my entire financial picture each month and was able to make better choices about the goals that were important to me. Suddenly it was obvious that success with money depended as much upon those choices as it did on the amount of my income. Being in charge of the choices was the answer. Once I saw where my money was going, it was easy to redirect it toward my goals: Eliminating credit card debt and starting a habit of saving money every month.

As I used the *Money Without Madness System* to reach my goals, my attitude about money changed. No longer did I complain about never having enough. Instead, I became responsible for managing the money that came to me and I *took action* to increase my income. Now I have a solid financial base and I understand my money. I have built upon it by adding investments, retirement planning, and acquisitions to the picture. My change in attitude affected my life as much as mastering my spending did.

OUR TRAINING

We all have money to handle. Most of us are never taught basic money skills as part of our upbringing or schooling. We are launched into jobs with the innocent assumption that our money needs no managing since no one ever told us what to do with it. It's not uncommon to supplement our income with credit card debt to meet our spending. We may want to save but can never find enough money to begin. It becomes a circle: How do we manage our money when we don't have enough of it and why don't we have enough money to manage?

THE ANSWER

Money Without Madness: Organize Your Budget and Stop Money Stress on Any Income is a step-by-step guide for you to add basic money skills, a positive attitude, and realistic financial goals to your life. It is written for people at all income levels who have no financial background, yet who are now prompted to unravel the mystery. *Money Without Madness* also includes topics not usually covered in a money book: Why traditional budget methods fail, and how to gracefully decline spending opportunities, decrease money stress, and keep your quality of life while reducing your quantity of spending.

Whether you want to attract more money into your life or let money take a back seat to other priorities, *Money Without Madness* provides practical solutions. Simply follow the steps at your own pace. By taking care of your money you take care of an important part of your life, and you will find your confidence and self-assurance increasing. As you relax and enjoy this change you will also discover a generous amount of new prosperity steadily filling your life.

—*Karen Brigham*

Introduction

Getting money, spending money, saving money, losing money, wanting money—money stress, money trouble, money fights—has money driven you mad lately? Is there a better way? YES! How about this: Plan your spending and control your money, gain credit card freedom and lose money stress, start saving now and improve your life immediately.

Money Without Madness: Organize Your Budget and Stop Money Stress on Any Income presents a new system for managing everyday money and everyday spending. The *Money Without Madness System* gives you three tools to change the way you deal with your money: your Spending Plan, your Money Mechanics, and your New Money Attitude. The goal of the *Money Without Madness System* is to bring three key money habits into your life:

1. *Manage your money monthly.*

2. *Gain credit card freedom.*

3. *Start saving now.*

That's it. That's all you need to focus on right now.

IT'S EASY

The system is easy to use since it takes advantage of several habits you probably already have. Do you spend all the cash in your wallet? Great! The *Money Without Madness System* requires you to do that. Are you the type of person who wants to deal with money only once a month and not think about it after that? The *Money Without Madness System* is designed for financial cruise control. Do you enjoy spontaneous spending instead of planning every penny? The *Money Without Madness System* provides for spontaneous spending and surprise expenses. And finally, do you toss your bills aside without even opening them, postponing the headache of dealing with them? Perfect, no need to change that habit either.

PLANNING TO SPEND

You don't need accounting knowledge to use the *Money Without Madness System* because it is not a technical system. Your own Spending Plan reflects your priorities in life—no one imposes spending rules on you. In Part One of the book, you'll become acquainted with the Spending Plan and create your own as you read through the chapters. You will learn how to use cash, checks, and credit cards to give you simplicity with your planning and flexibility with your spending. You'll see why you don't need to track the money you spend every week on food, entertainment, gas, lunches, and drugstore items, and you'll learn how to handle emergency expenses. Part One also teaches you to use credit cards for convenience and financial freedom instead of funding your standard of living, and it gives you ideas to help you start your *Saving Habit* now.

WHAT IS MONEY MECHANICS?

The *Money Without Madness System* streamlines your financial housekeeping into one monthly routine called your Money Mechanics. Part Two gives you tips on how to balance your checkbook in ten minutes and arrange to pay your bills at one time, quickly and correctly so you can then forget them. By adding two valuable steps—finishing *last* month's Spending Plan and creating *next* month's Spending Plan—you transform ordinary information into a monthly action plan to reach your financial goals. The process takes only two to three hours to complete and puts you on autopilot until next month. Well worth it, don't you agree?

AND WHAT ABOUT . . .

Planning ahead when your income is unpredictable? Does the *Money Without Madness System* work for couples? Have you ever thought about giving some of your money away? And, where do taxes fit into your Spending Plan? These topics are covered in Part Three, Making the Most of Your Money.

GOALS TO GROW BY

Conflicting money goals can raise questions about how to start. Should you pay off your credit cards first, or start saving for yourself? How do you balance today's spending requirements with future goal achievements? Part Four offers *The Twelve Steps to Financial Freedom*, a checklist to take you from wherever you are now to where you want to be—happily settled into the three key money habits. Attempting further financial ambitions makes no sense until the three key money habits are a solid part of your life. Getting there requires two things—knowledge and action. *Money Without Madness* gives you the knowledge you need in an easy-to-follow format. You decide how much to apply and at what pace to make the changes. Whether it takes you one year or five, the sooner you start working on *The Twelve Steps to Financial Freedom,* the sooner you make room for more money in your life.

BREAKING THE STRESS CYCLE

Your attitude about money has more impact on your money satisfaction than you may think. Stress caused by high debt and no savings is compounded by a poor money attitude. Worry, greed, and guilt get in the way of maximum money enjoyment and smooth progress toward your goals.

A critical part of the *Money Without Madness System* is retooling your old money attitudes as you make changes in your life. Replacing these attitudes with healthy doses of positive ideas and a new vocabulary is not only fun but necessary for a complete money overhaul. Part Four continues with ideas for new words to use that will help you relax and enjoy the money in your life. You also learn to use positive statements to decline spending opportunities and to reinforce your commitment to your financial progress, as well as strategies to keep you going when you feel overwhelmed.

ADDITIONAL RESOURCES

You'll find a list of Prosperity Books for further reading in Appendix A, two forms you'll need in Appendix B, and two indexes for quick and easy referral to specific topics and ideas.

SUMMARY

The following chapters show you how to organize your cash flow so you can make better choices with the money you have. The more you know about your money, the more your money will do for you. The more you enjoy the money you have now, the more new money will find its way to you. *Money Without Madness* replaces stress, worry, and madness about money with ease and confidence with your finances. *Money Without Madness* is the answer to the question, "How can I feel good about the money in my life?"

Turn the page and find out!

Part One

A Spending Plan that Works for You

The purpose of using a Spending Plan is to let you spend without guilt. There are four ways to use the Spending Plan form. First, you'll create a Master Spending Plan to get yourself used to the form and to spending your money in this new, organized way. Your Master Spending Plan shows your inflows and outflows for an average month using assumptions if needed, rather than specifics. This first step reveals what changes you may want to make in your life if you need extra money to reach your financial goals.

Since there are no average months, you'll revise and update your Master Spending Plan each month, using the specific details of that month's bills and spending. Maybe this is the month the kids need school clothes, or the dog gets his shots.

With these simple changes, your Master Spending plan becomes your Actual Spending Plan, the tool to turn theory into reality on a monthly basis.

At the end of each month, you'll review last month's spending, writing in the amounts you actually spent next to the amounts you planned to spend. This provides valuable feedback about what you did well and what you want to improve. That feedback goes into next month's Actual Spending Plan.

Additionally, you can use your Master Spending Plan as a "What If?" tool for setting future goals. "What if I add a car payment each month, took guitar lessons, or started automatic deductions for my savings?" "What if I took in a roommate, got a second job, or asked for (and received) a 10% raise this year?" Create a new Master Spending Plan with these assumptions, then set them as goals if they inspire you.

Let's dive right into the heart of the matter by walking you through the details of the Spending Plan. The *Money Without Madness* Spending Plan is different from any traditional budget you've seen or tried before. The concepts are simplified to make them basic, easy, and workable. Get some paper and a pencil before you start so you can develop your own plan as you read through this section.

Chapter One

Why You Need a Master Spending Plan

> *Those who fail to plan, plan to fail.*
> —Well-known business proverb
>
> *Those who plan to spend, succeed!*
> —Karen Brigham

DO YOU HAVE TO BUDGET?

Traditional budgets don't work. They are merely guessing games requiring a lot of tracking and totaling. All they tell you is whether or not you guessed correctly. They don't help you take action during the month, unless you track and total your expenses on a weekly basis. No one keeps that up for long! Traditional budgets lay out numerous categories and expect you to spend within the amount you allotted in each category. Not only is this difficult—it's not necessary. Only two things happen to your money—it stays or it leaves. Traditional budgets are information systems only. They tell you the barn door is open after the horse is gone. You don't need outdated information, you need instant feedback. You don't need rigid categories, you need flexibility. No, you don't have to budget—you need to *plan your spending*. The closer you follow your plan, the faster you'll gain control of your money.

NEW APPROACH—NEW NAME

Since we need a *plan* to manage our *spending,* let's call it that—a Spending Plan. Your *Master* Spending Plan gives you the overview of your financial picture with some ideal assumptions, and your *Actual* Spending Plan works with the actual details of each month's cash flow. And you guessed it—the forms are the same! You learn it once and you've got it twice.

WHAT IS IT?

Right now, take a look at the sample Spending Plan to see what we're talking about. It's all on one page, and it's not complicated. At the top you list your monthly income. After that, you list your expenses. The expenses are broken into five simple payment categories: CHECKS, which you write once a month when you pay your bills; CASH, which covers your repetitive weekly spending (no further tracking required); and FLEXIBLE MONEY, which covers all other spending. After those items are taken care of you'll use the next two categories, CREDIT CARD FREEDOM and START SAVING NOW! to plan the amount of money you'll spend each month in those two areas. We'll go over the Spending Plan in more detail in the following chapters so you'll be comfortable with it. As we do, you'll supply the relevant information from your own life to create your Master Spending Plan.

HOW DOES IT WORK?

The basic concept of the Spending Plan is simple—you subtract your monthly expenses from your monthly income. If the difference is positive, you decide what to do with the extra money. If it is negative, you figure out how to make it positive. When you create your Master Spending Plan you will estimate the amounts you don't know. When you work with your Actual Spending Plan, you'll use exact amounts because they will be available. After finishing your Master Spending Plan you'll see

SPENDING PLAN for Bella Femme

Month/Yr _____ End Date _____ No./Weeks _____

INCOME			Plan	Actual	Diff.
	Date	Amount			
Net Pay	_____	_____			
Other	_____		_____	_____	
Bottom Line —Last Month Surplus			_____	_____	
TOTAL INCOME			☐	☐	☐

EXPENSES		Plan	Actual	Diff.
Bottom Line-Last Month Negative		☐	☐	
Checks				
	House Payment	_____	_____	
	Car Payment	_____	_____	
	Donations	_____	_____	
	Phone	_____	_____	
	Utilities	_____	_____	
	Health Club	_____	_____	
	Hair & Beauty	_____	_____	
	_____	_____	_____	
	_____	_____	_____	
Total Checks		☐	☐	☐
Cash $_____ x _____		☐	☐	☐
dollars weeks				
Flexible Money _____		_____	_____	
_____		_____	_____	
Total Flexible Money		☐	☐	☐
Credit Card Freedom				
_____		_____	_____	
_____		_____	_____	
_____		_____	_____	
Total Credit Card Freedom		☐	☐	☐
Start Saving Now! YES!		☐	☐	☐
TOTAL EXPENSES		☐	☐	☐

BOTTOM LINE	Plan	Actual	Diff.
(Income minus expenses)	☐	☐	☐

whether your money situation needs a minor tune-up or a major overhaul.

Each month you'll use your Actual Spending Plan in two ways: first, to record your actual spending on the Spending Plan from the month just finished, and second, to prepare a new Spending Plan for the upcoming month. The first two columns, labeled PLAN and ACTUAL are for these numbers. The third column, DIFFERENCE, highlights the categories in which your actual spending may differ from what you planned. Going through this process each month allows you to become familiar with the exact amounts of income and expenses in your life, and see how they all work together.

WHAT'S IN A NAME?

To a dietitian the word "diet" means one thing, to me it means hunger—so forget it. Similarly, the word "budget" is frequently used to mean "economize" as in "We can't buy it now, we're trying to *budget.*" For anyone who has already attempted budgeting the word is likely to bring up feelings of failure. To some it carries regretful overtones of denial and sacrifice or describes a device used only as a temporary measure and last resort. With these unfavorable meanings attached to the word, we are off to a bad start if we use this negative name at all. Use Spending Plan, Cash Flow Plan, or create a name you like better. Avoid old terminology and you'll feel better about your new approach.

INTRODUCTIONS

Before going further, I'd like you to meet Bella Femme. Bella is a pretty woman, of French and Italian descent, who works at the cosmetics counter of a fine department store. Bella has agreed to be our example exemplar, our role model, as we go through the details of the Spending Plan (Thank you, Bella). Bella is twenty-five years old and single. She's been unsuccessful with past attempts to manage her money, so now she's motivated to make a positive change in her life once and for all. Bella will join us again after the next chapter.

FEARS, TEARS, AND CHEERS

Are you now experiencing a slight—or perhaps strong—resistance to some of this? Since this is a common roadblock, let's address the uncertainties behind this reaction.

I Won't Have Enough

"If I create a Spending Plan, I won't have as much money to spend as I used to, or want to." If you have this feeling, think for a minute: Can you really change the quantity of money you receive by writing it down? Will you have less by *knowing* what you have and where you want it to go? Understand that writing down where your money went and where you plan to spend it next month, *cannot* take money away from you. Understand that there's no way you can *have less* simply by looking at what you have.

I Don't Have Enough

"I make only a small amount of money. Why bother?" *You* are the person who will *most benefit* from careful organization of your cash flow. The less you bring in, the *more* important it is to get the best use from each dollar. It is critical for you to gain control over your money because you have no room for error. If you want to get more money, you need to first take responsibility for the money you have now. Once you do, you'll be ready to enjoy greater wealth as it comes to you.

No Spending Freedom

"If I write down where I plan to spend my money, I won't be able to spend spontaneously, and I'll feel guilty about blowing money." Not true if you *plan* to spend a certain amount of money freely on unknowns. When you *plan* for spontaneity, you are free to spend money on anything you want, without a trace of guilt, because you know it's part of your Spending Plan.

It's Too Complicated

"You're telling me this is easy, but it's starting to look complicated to me already. I'm not sure it's something I can do." Keep reading and be sure to create your own Master Spending Plan as you follow along. Once you start using the form, it will make sense to you. Allow yourself plenty of time for the information to sink in. If you still feel overwhelmed after a few chapters, read Chapter 25, From Anxiety to Excitement. This provides strategies to overcome doubts that may come up while using the *Money Without Madness System.*

I'd Rather Not Know

"If I look at the actual numbers I'll find out how far I am from where I want to be, and maybe I'd rather not know." This is the same fear that keeps some people from going to the doctor when they experience pain. They don't want to know how bad it might be. Face this fear head on. Consider this: Sooner or later you have to look at the facts of your financial situation. Eventually you will want to know the truth about getting from where you are to where you want to be. Learning to manage your money is the quickest way to make that journey. The longer you put it off, the more likely the remedy will be tougher. Face it now.

On The Other Hand . . .

One immediate benefit most people discover after completing their first Master Spending Plan is that things *aren't* as dismal as they previously thought. It's likely you are in this group.

What a relief to see your basic needs are easily covered by your income and the remainder of your money is merely slipping away without direction. With a few simple changes in the way you *manage* your spending, you will reach higher financial goals in no time.

STAY WITH IT

Your Spending Plan is a tool to help you add financial prosperity, and the goodies that go with it, to your life. In order for this tool to help at all, you need to use your Spending Plan once a month. This continues even when you find you haven't followed your Spending Plan and have overspent. It took me two years of *creating* Spending Plans each month before I could honestly report I was able to *follow* them. Better luck to you, but don't give up if you overspend on a consistent basis. As a matter of fact, expect it. The point of working with the Spending Plan is to quantify your overspending and carry the correction into next month's Spending Plan. On months when you *under*spend (there will be some, believe me!) you carry the *extra* money into next month's Spending Plan. Either way, using your Spending Plan helps you manage your money to meet your financial goals.

SUMMARY

If you've ever tried to budget in the past and it didn't work, you can throw out all unfavorable memories now. Traditional budgets are cumbersome and ineffective guessing games. You aren't going to budget anyone or anything. You aren't going to track every penny you spend. You *are* going to *plan your spending* so you move forward with a calm sense of knowing it all works. You will do this as long as you want prosperity in your life. It's part of the fun of having money. Welcome it and get used to it!

TAKE ACTION

ACTION ITEMS are listed at the end of each chapter. As you progress through the book, jot down the ACTION ITEMS you want to complete. Or, highlight the ones that apply to you directly on the chapter pages. When you're done with the book, you're ready to Take Action!

• Make twenty copies of the blank Spending Plan at the back of the book so you will have plenty for your first year.

Chapter Two

Do You Know _How_ You Spend Your Money?

> _That money talks I'll not deny,_
> _I heard it once: It said, 'Good-bye.'_
> —Richard Armour

Aside from robbery and taxes (one and the same?) there are only _three ways_ your hard earned funds can leave you: cash, check, and charge. This is the beauty of today's monetary system—it has devised only _three_ holes in your pocket.

This is great news! It means with just a tiny shift in _how you pay_ for your purchases you narrow the focus of your Spending Plan and simplify your spending. First, block one escape route completely by using credit cards _only occasionally_ for convenience and to shift emergency payments from one month to the next. Second, open another exit door a little wider by using cash to pay for your weekly repetitive costs (gas, lunches, entertainment, dry cleaning, etc.) more than you may do now. This will cut down on unnecessary tracking. With these changes in place you'll use fewer checks throughout the month, so each one will be the result of a conscious spending choice. With the _Money Without Madness System_ you think about _how_ you pay for something instead of _how much_ you pay for it. Using cash, checks, and credit cards in specific ways for your spending gives you a clear focus on where your money is going.

CASH—CHECK—CHARGE

Let's repeat this to let it sink in. Your weekly repetitive expenses and small miscellaneous purchases are covered with a constant amount of weekly cash. The rest of the items—bills, credit card payments, savings, and any remaining purchases—are paid with checks. You use your credit card only occasionally as a cash management tool *to shift unexpected payments from this month to the next.* This is the essence of keeping your Spending Plan simple and easy to follow. You'll see how in the next few chapters.

SUMMARY

Remember the three ways money escapes you are:

Cash—Check—Charge

To successfully limit the escape of money from your pockets, use your Spending Plan to watch these three exit doors. Your money no longer stands a chance of leaving without permission or sneaking out without a trail. Those days are over! You are on the alert now for dollars on the loose!

TAKE ACTION

- Check your pockets for money-sized holes. Make sure there are only three.

Chapter Three

Keep Track of Your Checkbook

It's easier to make money than to keep it.

—Jewish proverb

There are a bunch of payments you make every month that do not vary much once you set yourself up with a certain lifestyle. These payments are the easiest to predict. So instead of starting with the first item on your Spending Plan (INCOME), let's start with the *easiest*—your fixed expenses. These are items you are usually billed for and you pay with checks. Remember, checks are one of the escape routes you're watching closely now.

Turn to you sample Spending Plan and find CHECKS listed under the title EXPENSES. (For now, ignore the first line under EXPENSES titled BOTTOM LINE—LAST MONTH NEGATIVE. We use that later on.) In the column titled PLAN next to the appropriate line, you will list the bills you receive every month. As we go through this first step, try to loosen any mental blocks you may have on this subject so you'll have a better chance of remembering them all.

MONTHLY EXPENSES

Start by listing the payments you make (or need to make) once a month to maintain your lifestyle. These include any of the following: house, car, utilities, phone, cable, health club dues, insurance, etc. List any others in the blanks. (Do not list credit card payments yet.) Use an estimate for those items that change in amount every month such as the phone and utility bills. Be sure you are generous (high enough) with your estimate.

Bella lists her expenses as follows:

Rent	$630	(shared rental house)
Car Payment	80	(Honda scooter)
Donations	50	(she's generous)
Telephone	60	(close friend in Seattle)
Utilities	25	(mild California climate)
Health Club	20	(good deal!)
CD Club	15	(small luxury)

Notice that Bella's numbers end in either five or zero. This is no coincidence; rather it's because she rounds the actual amounts up or down to make them easier to work with. As you complete your Spending Plan, ignore pennies and round up or down to the nearest five or ten dollars. Rounding has many benefits we'll cover later in Chapter 16, Creative Rounding Saves You Time.

LESS THAN MONTHLY

Next, list any payments you make less than once a month by breaking them into monthly portions. For example, if you make quarterly payments for health insurance or estimated tax payments, divide the number by three to get a monthly total. If you own a home and pay property taxes, break that amount into a monthly figure. Again, these are payments that are not optional with your current lifestyle. For Bella, this includes the cost of maintaining the *natural* strawberry blonde color of her hair.

Hair & Beauty $30   (normally $60 at the salon
every other month)

MORE THAN MONTHLY

Next, write down any payments you make more than once a month by check although you do not receive a bill for them. These may include music lessons, counseling fees, church donations, day care expenses, etc. For families, this may include checks for weekly groceries. Typically, the amount is constant. Bella has entertainment ambitions and takes voice lessons. She goes every other week and pays $20 per lesson.

Voice $40

Take your checkbook out to help you recall these expenses. What bills have you paid over the last several months that will continue in future months? Bella finds checks for food, but the amounts are not constant and predictable. Sometimes she eats out or at her parents' house rather than at home. She'll exclude this for now since the amounts vary so much. She also spends money periodically for clothes. Since this isn't a constant and predictable expense, she won't list it here.

TOTAL IT UP

Now total these expenses and put the sum in the box across from the words TOTAL CHECKS. These expenses are constant and recurring. You have little or no control over spending this money without making a change in your lifestyle. The

SPENDING PLAN for Bella Femme

Month/Yr _Master_   End Date _____   No./Weeks _____

INCOME			Plan	Actual	Diff.
Net Pay	Date _____	Amount _____			
Other	_____	_____	_____	_____	
Bottom Line —Last Month Surplus			_____	_____	
TOTAL INCOME			☐	☐	☐

EXPENSES		Plan	Actual	Diff.
Bottom Line -Last Month Negative		☐	☐	
Checks				
	House Payment	630	_____	
	Car Payment	80	_____	
	Donations	50	_____	
	Phone	60	_____	
	Utilities	25	_____	
	Health Club	20	_____	
	Hair & Beauty	30	_____	
	CD Club	15	_____	
	Voice	40	_____	
Total Checks		950	☐	☐
Cash $_____ x _____		☐	☐	☐
dollars weeks				
Flexible Money _____		_____	_____	
		_____	_____	
Total Flexible Money		☐	☐	☐
Credit Card Freedom				
_____		_____	_____	
_____		_____	_____	
_____		_____	_____	
Total Credit Card Freedom		☐	☐	☐
Start Saving Now! YES!		☐	☐	☐
TOTAL EXPENSES		☐	☐	☐

BOTTOM LINE	Plan	Actual	Diff.
(Income minus expenses)	☐	☐	☐

monthly total will not change much unless you move to a different apartment, sell your car, enlist in a super-deluxe health club, etc. Two exceptions are your phone and utility bills, which obviously vary depending on use. Bella's total equals $950. She uses a calculator and adds twice to make sure she has done it correctly.

A WORD ON PRIORITIES

You may have heard the advice, pay yourself *first.* This means make a payment to your own savings before paying your bills. I tried this and was unsuccessful. For me, there is value in having a roof over my head so making that payment is important to me. The same holds true for *all* my fixed expenses. They represent things I've included in my life by choice, so why risk losing them by not paying for them? I could delay the payments if I wanted to, but the hassle of late notices and complaints are an irritant I'm reluctant to sign up for. I prefer to modify my lifestyle or increase my income, so I pay on time for everything and *also* have money left to pay myself.

SUMMARY

The bulk of your money is spent on predictable payments that maintain life as you know it. These costs are simple to manage when you use checks every month to cover them. The total won't vary much unless you make a major change in your lifestyle.

You've now completed one of the sections of your Spending Plan. Wasn't it easy? Now what about those disappearing small dollars that can add up to so much? How do we control them? Onward!

TAKE ACTION

- Buy a three-ring binder in your favorite color to keep your Spending Plans organized.

- Invest in a three-hole punch.

- Buy some pencils. Use these for your Spending Plans until you are a pro and want to use a pen.

Chapter Four

Make Sure You Have Extra Cash to Spend

With your feet in the oven, and your head in the freezer, on average you're comfortable.

—Professor of statistics

Money burns a hole in *my* pocket, how about yours? I used to cash a check whenever I got paid and be so happy to have money to spend, I'd go on a spree and immediately be broke again. I remember asking myself why I never seemed to have enough money to buy just the simple drugstore items everyone needs or a reasonable variety of food at the grocery store. I'd find myself in a poverty mode until the next paycheck—usually two weeks away—and I didn't understand why. Of course, as soon as I got the next paycheck I had a backlog of items to buy. So off I'd go, feeling anxious but still spending all my money. Broke again, I'd wait for the next paycheck and start the cycle all over.

What a way to live—paycheck to paycheck! Finally, I made an easy but significant change. I gave myself a weekly amount of Cash to Burn and stuck to it. Instead of living from one paycheck to the next according to someone else's schedule, I lived from week to week on an amount *I chose* to give myself. This gave me control over my money. Eventually my life became financially steady instead of swinging wildly from poverty to plenty and back again. I went from big spending binges every two weeks, to smaller ones every week, and ultimately to a steady state. Once I got used to spending the same amount every week, it worked automatically.

CASH TO BURN

The next thing you need to think about is how much cash you'll want to burn on a weekly basis. You may need to use $20 increments if that's what your automated teller machine (ATM) gives you. As you start thinking about this, let's go over the items your weekly cash covers. These will be small, recurring purchases you make every week or every other week and are not worth the effort of tracking. Larger, infrequent purchases (car repairs, appliances, kids' clothing, CD players, furniture, etc.) are covered later.

Entertainment

This can be anything you want it to be, as long as it entertains you. It always comes out of your Cash to Burn. When you plan to eat, drink, and be merry, keep an eye on your wallet and leave some cash for the upcoming event.

Drugstore

All drugstore purchases come out of Cash to Burn. When you have more cash available, stock up. When you have less, buy the minimum amount of items and plan to stock up next week. Next week is always only a few days away, so it's easy to wait.

Lunches

If you eat out for lunch you probably already set aside a weekly amount of cash, and you know how much that is. Include this amount in your Cash to Burn.

Dry Cleaning/Shoe Repair

These payments come out of your Cash to Burn, especially if they occur frequently and are small amounts. If they aren't, make your trips over a period of weeks to smooth the spending and ease it into your weekly cash amount.

Car Washes

Whenever you frequent the car wash, use your Cash to Burn.

Food

If you vary your eating between restaurant meals and home-cooked goodies, your Cash to Burn covers all food. If you buy groceries weekly because you eat regularly at home or because you have a family to feed, you may want to consider groceries an item to pay by check and include a monthly amount for it in the CHECKS category. Then your weekly Cash to Burn covers dinners out only.

Gas

Fill the tank at least once a week whether you need to or not. That way you do it when you have the money and time instead of being caught inconveniently low on gas (and perhaps cash). Your Cash to Burn covers gas unless you charge *all* your gas, then include the payment for your gas charge card under CHECKS. The monthly amount won't vary much.

Other

All small purchases of miscellaneous items come from your weekly Cash to Burn. By small I mean, under $30. When you first start, you'll notice a surprisingly large number of miscellaneous items. Use your cash for these, keeping in mind your goal of using the same amount of cash each week. Add an extra $20, or more, to your tally of Cash to Burn to cover these items.

ADD IT UP

Take a moment now to calculate your amount of weekly Cash to Burn. Bella figures hers this way:

Entertainment	$15	
Drugstore	10	
Lunches	0	(Bella packs her lunch and eats in the employee lunchroom)
Dry Cleaning	0	(This doesn't happen too often so she'll take it from Other cash—see below)
Car Washes	0	(Ditto)
Grocery Food	30	
Gas	15	
Other	<u>30</u>	(This is a guess for now)

Total Cash to Burn: $100 per week

WHATEVER YOUR HEART DESIRES

Although you use these estimates to calculate a weekly total, remember you are free to spend the cash any way you like. You may spend it all on a glittery night on the town and eat crackers for the rest of the week if you want. It is your choice! But spend it. It's good for your soul and for the economy.

SMOOTH SPENDING

A word about bulk buying and other economy purchases. Bulk buying appeals to a lot of people because the unit price is attractive. If you like to make bulk buys and can do it *with-*

SPENDING PLAN for Bella Femme

Month/Yr ___Master___ End Date _____ No./Weeks _____4_____

INCOME			Plan	Actual	Diff.
Net Pay	Date	Amount			
Other					
Bottom Line —Last Month Surplus					
TOTAL INCOME			☐	☐	☐

EXPENSES		Plan	Actual	Diff.
Bottom Line -Last Month Negative		☐	☐	
Checks				
	House Payment	630	_____	
	Car Payment	80	_____	
	Donations	50	_____	
	Phone	60	_____	
	Utilities	25	_____	
	Health Club	20	_____	
	Hair & Beauty	30	_____	
	CD Club	15	_____	
	Voice	40	_____	
Total Checks		950	☐	☐
Cash $___100___ x _____ dollars weeks		☐	☐	☐
Flexible Money _____		_____	_____	
		_____	_____	
Total Flexible Money		☐	☐	☐
Credit Card Freedom				
_____		_____	_____	
_____		_____	_____	
_____		_____	_____	
Total Credit Card Freedom		☐	☐	☐
Start Saving Now! YES!		☐	☐	☐
TOTAL EXPENSES		☐	☐	☐

BOTTOM LINE	Plan	Actual	Diff.
(Income minus expenses)	☐	☐	☐

out going over your weekly amount of cash—fine. Do it! But don't use it as a reason to take out extra cash. The logic goes something like this: "I can buy enough paper towels now to last three months and save money on the total price, so it's a good purchase. Over the next three months I won't spend any money buying paper towels, so my outflow is less." Theoretically, you have saved money. However, if you spend an extra $40 now over your usual cash amount, you are *not* going to deduct approximately three dollars a week over the next three months from your Cash to Burn without getting far more complicated than you want to. You are more likely to spend the extra $40 now *and* spend the savings on something else down the road. The result is you spend more *in total* than you otherwise would. When faced with a bulk buy without the cash to pay for it, stick with your cash plan. The idea is to smooth your spending into a constant amount each week. However, you may write a check from your Flexible Money to purchase your bulk buys. More on that later.

Tip: Gradually stock up on any items you go through quickly, and *must have immediately* when you run out: contact lens solution, paper towels, soap, pet food, popcorn, dental floss. The next time you run out, refill from your supply and buy at your leisure rather than immediately. This way you manage your emergency purchases instead of them managing you.

PAYDAY!

Pick a cash payday for yourself. Stick to it every week. Pick a day that works well with your weekly schedule. I get my cash on Friday and use it the next morning for my weekly round of errands: gas, drugstore, and groceries. A disadvantage is that if I don't do my errands on Saturday, I usually wind up spending the money on other weekend enjoyments and live a pretty lean week until next Friday (but what a weekend!). Also, since many people get paid on Fridays, the likelihood of waiting in line at the ATM is about one hundred percent. I sometimes think Monday might be a better payday since I'm busy at work all week and less likely to spend my money immediately.

SHORT ON CASH?

When you first give yourself a weekly amount of cash, you may run out at times. If this happens a lot, your amount of weekly cash may not be high enough. Don't be too lean with this money. If you constantly run out, you will feel broke and start resenting the whole plan. Better to be reasonable and know it's working. Occasionally you will still run out of cash. To accommodate this, simply borrow from next week. Take an extra $20 this week when you've unexpectedly run out, and remember to take $20 *less* next week. At the end of the month you'll be right on target.

NO COUNTING

It doesn't matter at all what you spend your Cash to Burn on, and you can make new choices each week. What matters is that you look to your wallet to guide your spending, a reliable habit most of us have already acquired. The beauty is there's no tracking, counting, and subtracting—your wallet does it for you. Look in your wallet, and if you don't like what you *don't* see, remember that it's only a matter of a few days until it will be full again.

INSTANT FEEDBACK

Your wallet gives you instant feedback. If you make a second trip to the ATM machine for an extra $20, you know you're in an overspending situation. There are times you'll choose to do this because something comes up that's more important than your Spending Plan. The choice is always yours to make, but it is a choice—not an accident.

SUMMARY

Your Cash to Burn covers your basic spending needs—it pays for your well-being. Test this amount over the next four weeks and make sure it's reasonable for you. Once you find the right weekly amount, think of it as a fixed expense and keep it constant. Over a period of time your spending will automatically adjust to that level and you'll appreciate the simplicity of a steady amount of money to count on.

DO IT

On your Spending Plan, write your weekly amount of Cash to Burn in the blank after the word CASH that is marked with a dollar sign ($). The next step is to multiply that amount by the number of weeks in a month to come up with a monthly Cash-to-Burn figure. The question is, *"How many weeks in a month?"* Read on . . .

TAKE ACTION

- Make a list of items you want to buy to accumulate an extra supply. Buy one each week until you have a full stock.

- Pick your cash payday.

- Try getting your weekly cash and buying gas, groceries, and drugstore items all in one trip. This way you pay for your necessities first, then relax while spending the rest of your cash during the week.

Chapter Five

Use a Calendar to Organize Your Spending

Them that makes the rules gets the gold.
—Street version of the Golden Rule

Do you find you get an extra paycheck every once in a while, out of the blue? Have you figured out there are more weeks in the year than evenly fit into twelve months? Many of your *expenses* occur monthly, but your paychecks may not coincide. What about your Cash to Burn, which you spend on a weekly basis? What do you do when a month ends midweek?

CHANGE THE CALENDAR

In the business world, companies facing this situation developed a new calendaring method called the *4-4-5* system. The method names the number of weeks per month in a three-month period. A three-month period (a quarter) always has the same number of weeks (thirteen) and each month ends on the same day of the week. This eases a number of corporate issues related to accounting periods, and it is the answer for your personal Spending Plans as well. If you're confused, read on. . . .

Under this system, the first two months of a quarter have four weeks each and the last month has five weeks. Then the pattern repeats. Using this calendar system, the year 2000 works like this:

The Year 2000

Month	Weeks	Last Day of Each Month
January	4	Friday, January 28
February	4	Friday, February 25
March	5	Friday, March 31
April	4	Friday, April 28
May	4	Friday, May 26
June	5	Friday, June 30
July	4	Friday, July 28
August	4	Friday, August 25
September	5	Friday, September 29
October	4	Friday, October 27
November	4	Friday, November 24
December	5	Friday, December 29

. . . and looks like the calendar on the next page.

Notice the *4-4-5* pattern of weeks. Of course, you are not changing the real calendar in any way, you are simply adopting a pattern that works better for your Spending Plan and coincides closely with the natural months of the calendar.

2000

JANUARY 2000

S	M	T	W	T	F	S
						1
2	3	4	5	6	7	8
9	10	11	12	13	14	15
16	17	18	19	20	21	22
23	24	25	26	27	28	29
30	31					

FEBRUARY 2000

S	M	T	W	T	F	S
		1	2	3	4	5
6	7	8	9	10	11	12
13	14	15	16	17	18	19
20	21	22	23	24	25	26
27	28	29				

MARCH 2000

S	M	T	W	T	F	S
			1	2	3	4
5	6	7	8	9	10	11
12	13	14	15	16	17	18
19	20	21	22	23	24	25
26	27	28	29	30	31	

APRIL 2000

S	M	T	W	T	F	S
						1
2	3	4	5	6	7	8
9	10	11	12	13	14	15
16	17	18	19	20	21	22
23	24	25	26	27	28	29
30						

MAY 2000

S	M	T	W	T	F	S
	1	2	3	4	5	6
7	8	9	10	11	12	13
14	15	16	17	18	19	20
21	22	23	24	25	26	27
28	29	30	31			

JUNE 2000

S	M	T	W	T	F	S
				1	2	3
4	5	6	7	8	9	10
11	12	13	14	15	16	17
18	19	20	21	22	23	24
25	26	27	28	29	30	

JULY 2000

S	M	T	W	T	F	S
						1
2	3	4	5	6	7	8
9	10	11	12	13	14	15
16	17	18	19	20	21	22
23	24	25	26	27	28	29
30	31					

AUGUST 2000

S	M	T	W	T	F	S
		1	2	3	4	5
6	7	8	9	10	11	12
13	14	15	16	17	18	19
20	21	22	23	24	25	26
27	28	29	30	31		

SEPTEMBER 2000

S	M	T	W	T	F	S
					1	2
3	4	5	6	7	8	9
10	11	12	13	14	15	16
17	18	19	20	21	22	23
24	25	26	27	28	29	30

OCTOBER 2000

S	M	T	W	T	F	S
1	2	3	4	5	6	7
8	9	10	11	12	13	14
15	16	17	18	19	20	21
22	23	24	25	26	27	28
29	30	31				

NOVEMBER 2000

S	M	T	W	T	F	S
			1	2	3	4
5	6	7	8	9	10	11
12	13	14	15	16	17	18
19	20	21	22	23	24	25
26	27	28	29	30		

DECEMBER 2000

S	M	T	W	T	F	S
					1	2
3	4	5	6	7	8	9
10	11	12	13	14	15	16
17	18	19	20	21	22	23
24	25	26	27	28	29	30
31						

2001

JANUARY 2001

S	M	T	W	T	F	S
	1	2	3	4	5	6
7	8	9	10	11	12	13
14	15	16	17	18	19	20
21	22	23	24	25	26	27
28	29	30	31			

FEBRUARY 2001

S	M	T	W	T	F	S
				1	2	3
4	5	6	7	8	9	10
11	12	13	14	15	16	17
18	19	20	21	22	23	24
25	26	27	28			

MARCH 2001

S	M	T	W	T	F	S
				1	2	3
4	5	6	7	8	9	10
11	12	13	14	15	16	17
18	19	20	21	22	23	24
25	26	27	28	29	30	31

APRIL 2001

S	M	T	W	T	F	S
1	2	3	4	5	6	7
8	9	10	11	12	13	14
15	16	17	18	19	20	21
22	23	24	25	26	27	28
29	30					

MAY 2001

S	M	T	W	T	F	S
		1	2	3	4	5
6	7	8	9	10	11	12
13	14	15	16	17	18	19
20	21	22	23	24	25	26
27	28	29	30	31		

JUNE 2001

S	M	T	W	T	F	S
					1	2
3	4	5	6	7	8	9
10	11	12	13	14	15	16
17	18	19	20	21	22	23
24	25	26	27	28	29	30

JULY 2001

S	M	T	W	T	F	S
1	2	3	4	5	6	7
8	9	10	11	12	13	14
15	16	17	18	19	20	21
22	23	24	25	26	27	28
29	30	31				

AUGUST 2001

S	M	T	W	T	F	S
			1	2	3	4
5	6	7	8	9	10	11
12	13	14	15	16	17	18
19	20	21	22	23	24	25
26	27	28	29	30	31	

SEPTEMBER 2001

S	M	T	W	T	F	S
						1
2	3	4	5	6	7	8
9	10	11	12	13	14	15
16	17	18	19	20	21	22
23	24	25	26	27	28	29
30						

OCTOBER 2001

S	M	T	W	T	F	S
	1	2	3	4	5	6
7	8	9	10	11	12	13
14	15	16	17	18	19	20
21	22	23	24	25	26	27
28	29	30	31			

NOVEMBER 2001

S	M	T	W	T	F	S
				1	2	3
4	5	6	7	8	9	10
11	12	13	14	15	16	17
18	19	20	21	22	23	24
25	26	27	28	29	30	

DECEMBER 2001

S	M	T	W	T	F	S
						1
2	3	4	5	6	7	8
9	10	11	12	13	14	15
16	17	18	19	20	21	22
23	24	25	26	27	28	29
30	31					

THE WEEK ENDS ON _____?

In our example, we chose Friday to be the last day of the week and therefore of each month. Your week can end on any day you like as long as you stay with that day. Coordinating the last day of your Spending Plan week with the day you receive your paycheck works well if you are paid weekly or biweekly. Since I receive my paycheck on Friday, the last day of my week works best as a Friday and the entire paycheck pays for the next two weeks.

GET SET

To set up your *4-4-5* calendar, get a calendar for the whole year (there's usually one on the back of your check register). Count out the number of full weeks for each month starting with four in both January and February (the first and second months), five in March (the third month), then repeat. Circle the last day of each of your new months, making sure you end within a couple of days of December 31. Keep this calendar where you can easily use it once a month. (The back of your check register or in your Spending Plan binder is perfect.) At the top of each Actual Spending Plan is a blank to write in the END DATE and the number of WEEKS. Fill these in when you do your Actual Spending Plans with the information from the *4-4-5* calendar you just finished.

The total Cash to Burn in your Actual Spending Plan is your weekly amount times the number of weeks in that month. Simple enough. Since this is your Master Spending Plan and you are not working with a specific month, use four weeks. Take a moment now to complete the **CASH** line on your Master Spending Plan. Bella's is easy—$100 times four weeks gives her a total of $400 each month for Cash to Burn. She puts that on her Master Spending Plan.

SPENDING PLAN *for Bella Femme*

Month/Yr ___Master___ End Date _____ No./Weeks ___4___

INCOME			Plan	Actual	Diff.
	Date	Amount			
Net Pay	_____	_____			
Other	_____	_____	_____	_____	
Bottom Line —Last Month Surplus			_____	_____	
TOTAL INCOME			☐	☐	☐

EXPENSES		Plan	Actual	Diff.
Bottom Line-Last Month Negative		☐	☐	
Checks				
	House Payment	630	_____	
	Car Payment	80	_____	
	Donations	50	_____	
	Phone	60	_____	
	Utilities	25	_____	
	Health Club	20	_____	
	Hair & Beauty	30	_____	
	CD Club	15	_____	
	Voice	40	_____	
Total Checks		950	☐	☐
Cash $___100___ x ___4___ dollars weeks		*400*	☐	☐
Flexible Money _____		_____	_____	
_____		_____	_____	
Total Flexible Money		☐	☐	☐
Credit Card Freedom				
_____		_____	_____	
_____		_____	_____	
_____		_____	_____	
Total Credit Card Freedom		☐	☐	☐
Start Saving Now! YES!		☐	☐	☐
TOTAL EXPENSES		☐	☐	☐

BOTTOM LINE	Plan	Actual	Diff.
(Income minus expenses)	☐	☐	☐

YOUR PAYCHECK

Calculating your monthly income with the new *4-4-5* calendar depends on how often your employer pays you. Many people get a check on a weekly or a biweekly basis. Both fit perfectly into the *4-4-5* system. If you are paid weekly, multiply your net pay by the number of weeks in the month you're working with (either four or five). If you get a check every other Friday, simply divide it in half, (one half for the first week *following* the check and one half for the second), then multiply. The paycheck you receive *now* pays for expenses belonging to the next week (or two weeks). It follows a logical sequence: You earn it, you get it, you spend it.

A PLEASANT SURPRISE

If this looks like more trouble than it's worth—*take the trouble.* There is a hidden benefit that makes it all worthwhile. What if you got an extra week of pay every three months for your trouble? A bonus. Would it be worth it? Most of us agree it would. How can this happen? In the examples above you've divided both your income and your months into weekly periods so they fit together. Since you've given yourself five weeks every third month, you get an extra week of pay. Your landlord doesn't charge you more rent that month and you don't receive another utility or phone bill. The only added expense for that extra week of pay is one week's worth of Cash to Burn, so the rest of the money is *all* yours!

FUN MONEY

Believe me, this little chunk of money comes in handy! You can count on receiving it every March, June, September, and December. You may use it for a large purchase (a piano), a small purchase (a diamond), or to pay for that wonderful weekend getaway with your sweetheart. You may use it for any unexpected payments that accumulate (we discuss this in

Chapter 6, Plan for Unexpected Expenses). I use mine to buy new clothes twice a year when the seasons and styles change. And in December (Happy Holidays!) we all know what the extra money goes for.

While it may seem like you've just created more money, unfortunately that's not the case. What you've created is a system telling you *when* you can expect to receive your extra bonus and how much it will be. Knowing you can *count* on it allows you to put it into your Spending Plan. To calculate your bonus amount, subtract one week's Cash to Burn from one week's take-home paycheck.

MONTHLY AND SEMIMONTHLY PAYCHECKS

If you are paid once or twice a month, planning your income is easy. You get the same amount every month. Those of you who are paid on the first of each month get all your income up front, which eases cash flow. If you are paid twice a month, you may need to wait until mid-month to release some checks for payment. You can simplify your cash flow with the following change: Count the last check received last month as the first check for income this month. For example, if you receive $1,000 on the tenth of each month and another $1,000 on the twentieth, list a total of $2,000 for income each month. For planning the month of April, the check received on March 20 is counted as the first $1,000 of *April's* income, and the check received on April 10 as the second $1,000 of April's income. This way, all the money is in your bank account by the tenth of each month. You can pay your bills any time after that. For May, the checks received on April 20 and May 10 are the income checks.

WATCH OUT

Those of you who receive monthly or semimonthly paychecks will have a *more expensive* third month of each quarter. Using the 4-4-5 system you have five weeks of Cash to Burn every third month but your monthly income stays the same. You can work around this two ways: (1) target any extra spending for the first and second months of every quarter and you'll be set; or, (2) calculate a *monthly* Cash to Burn amount, divide it in half, and take that amount from your ATM on the first and fifteenth of each month, instead of every week. If you are paid twice a month, this coincides with each paycheck.

DO IT

If you receive a weekly or biweekly paycheck, calculate four weeks' worth of take-home pay and put the total on one of the lines labeled NET PAY in the INCOME section of your Spending Plan. If you are paid monthly or semimonthly, put the monthly amount in that spot.

If you receive commissions or another type of income that fluctuates in amount, estimate a monthly total you can reasonably expect to receive and put the amount in the INCOME section. Be sure to read Chapter 17, Planning with Unpredictable Income, which provides more detail on working with fluctuating incomes.

OTHER INCOME

Include amounts for other income you receive in the INCOME section under OTHER. If you receive quarterly income such as dividends, divide the amount by three and list it now. If you receive small, occasional income (baby-sitting, gifts, garage sale money) it is best to exclude it from your Master Spending Plan since it is not reliable. If the income is steady and reliable (housecleaning money, child support payments), go ahead and include it on your Master Spending Plan so you can plan to spend it.

Total your monthly income and put the total in the box titled TOTAL INCOME.

SPENDING PLAN for Bella Femme

Month/Yr ___Master___   End Date _____   No./Weeks ___4___

INCOME			Plan	Actual	Diff.
Net Pay	Date _____	Amount 750			
	_____	750	1,500	_____	
Other			_____	_____	
Bottom Line —Last Month Surplus			_____	_____	
TOTAL INCOME			1,500		

EXPENSES		Plan	Actual	Diff.
Bottom Line-Last Month Negative				
Checks				
	House Payment	630	_____	
	Car Payment	80	_____	
	Donations	50	_____	
	Phone	60	_____	
	Utilities	25	_____	
	Health Club	20	_____	
	Hair & Beauty	30	_____	
	CD Club	15	_____	
	Voice	40	_____	
Total Checks		950		
Cash $___100___ x ___4___ dollars weeks		400		
Flexible Money _____				
_____				
Total Flexible Money				
Credit Card Freedom				
_____				
_____				
_____				
Total Credit Card Freedom				
Start Saving Now! YES!				
TOTAL EXPENSES				

BOTTOM LINE	Plan	Actual	Diff.
(Income minus expenses)			

Bella estimates her monthly commissions, after taxes are deducted, to be around $1,500 and lists that amount on her Spending Plan. She expects no other regular income—no healthy dividends, portfolio interest, mutual fund distributions, gambling winnings, or business profits . . . not yet!

SUMMARY

You may not be able to *change* the calendar or the dates you receive your paycheck; however, you can *customize* the calendar to match your spending weeks. Now your paychecks easily fit your new calendar! Before you know it, you have a predictable, manageable system designed to make your Spending Plan work.

TAKE ACTION

- Create your *4-4-5* calendar for the remainder of the year.

- Calculate your weekly income amount if you are paid weekly or biweekly.

- Calculate the bonus amount you'll get each quarter.

Chapter Six

Plan for Unexpected Expenses

> *The heaviest weight in the world is an empty pocket.*
>
> —Folk saying

What about expenses we haven't yet mentioned? Those that don't come up *every month* but come up sooner or later: clothing, a VCR, gifts, medical and dental bills, a new CD player, tax preparation fees, a microwave oven, car registration fees, etc.?

You must plan to cover these expenses, or your Spending Plan isn't realistic. The most common reason many Spending Plans fail, both in personal lives and business enterprises, is because little or no provision is made for unknowns. Month after month, expenses turn up that aren't planned for and money is spent to cover them. The result? Spending over the original plan. Some people try to curb spontaneous spending, which may work in the short term but catches up to them in the long term.

COUNT ON IT

Since you *know* some amount of unforeseen expenses will occur, you simply need to *plan for them*. Each month you'll allow a sum of money to cover three types of unplanned expenses: desires, emergencies, and spontaneous spending. Since the priority and price of these expenses vary from month to month, flexibility is essential in managing this money. One month a speeding ticket is your highest priority. The next month a radar detector is high on your list of purchases. Because flexibility is the key to using this money successfully, it is listed on your Spending Plan as FLEXIBLE MONEY.

PLAN THE PURCHASE OR PLAN THE PAYMENT

Two approaches work well for spending this money: Plan the Purchase, or Plan the Payment. The idea is to keep the total spending in your Flexible Money on target by juggling your priorities within this category every month. When you know about a purchase in advance, you'll *plan the purchase* for a month with enough Flexible Money to cover it. When an emergency arises, you'll *plan the payment* to fit into future months' Flexible Money. This can be done either by working out a payment plan or by using your credit card. Read on for more details on these approaches.

WANTON WANTING

Everyone makes miscellaneous purchases that vary from month to month and are not true emergencies, but are simply items you desire (artwork, ski passes, massages, a camcorder, power tools, tickets to a concert, samba dance lessons, etc.). These are items you *want*, that you are just *dying* to have, but that may not be *required* this month. It's important to provide Flexible Money for some of these purchases each month, or you deprive yourself instead of taking care of yourself.

When all these purchases are covered easily by the Flexible Money available to you in the month you want to buy them—great! Do it! If your wanting goes beyond the Flexible Money available to you in one month, start a Want List. Every time you think of something you want, write it down with a price estimate. Don't lowball yourself on this estimate or you'll end up spending more and discourage yourself by thinking you overspent. It's better to estimate the amount realistically and have money left as a nice surprise. At the beginning of each month, look at your Want List and decide which items you'll buy. List them on your Spending Plan in the FLEXIBLE MONEY category.

Creating a Want List focuses your spending on items you still want after the initial urge has passed. It is satisfying to *do something* with your desires, even if it is simply writing them down. As money becomes available, it is destined to be spent on meaningful purchases rather than to disappear quickly on impulse buys. Whenever you find yourself thinking "I wish I had _____ ," write it down! The more you write down, the better. After using your Want List for a while, you'll look back and see how many items you have purchased and crossed off. When you are diligent about using your Want List, it is truly only a matter of time before you will buy everything you want.

SWIFT SHIFTING—PLAN THE PAYMENT

Credit cards are great tools to shift payments from one month to the next. This is an important benefit a credit card provides, and it's why you should never be without one. You don't have to pay for a major emergency *right now* and blow your current month's Spending Plan. Instead, you postpone the payment until you get your credit card bill and work it into next month's Spending Plan. If you pay the amount in full, this convenience costs you nothing. If you choose not to pay the full amount, you will pay interest until the balance is zero. Don't let that bother you. True emergencies can't be predicted and many can't be prevented. When one occurs, your life may be interrupted from its usual course in many respects. Extra cost is just one of them. It's better to take your time with an emergency payment, even at additional cost, than to add to your troubles by skimping on the rest of your money and therefore your well-being. Credit cards allow you this convenience. You may not be able to control the emergency, but you can control the payment by using your credit card.

UNIDENTIFIED SPONTANEOUS SPENDING

How boring life would be without any spontaneous spending! Some opportunities arise now, then are gone. You don't want to miss them because you didn't first list them on your Want List or Spending Plan. Many of these are social opportunities: dinner with friends, tickets to a hockey game, a hot date on Friday night, a ski trip, etc. If you don't want to pass up these enticing occasions, be sure to leave some money unidentified in your Flexible Money category every month for truly spontaneous spending. Opportunities arise and you'll want to go for them!

TRACK IT DOWN

The beauty of the *Money Without Madness System* is that your Flexible Money amount is the *only number to remember* each month. Once you know how much it is, put it on a Post-it™ note on your checkbook register. Any time you purchase something from this category, deduct it from the total and keep a running total on the note. That way, you always know how much Flexible Money is left, and you prevent accidental overspending. As long as you keep track of this number and use the same amount of Cash to Burn each week, your Spending Plan will come out on target every month. It's that simple.

Use checks, or a debit card, to pay for your Flexible Money purchases. Since this is the only time you'll write a check after paying your bills, you'll know exactly where the money is coming from and if it's available. At the end of the month, you'll know how you spent your Flexible Money by listing all your checks, or debit deductions, and totaling them. An exception: If you need more cash one week for some small-dollar spontaneous spending, make a trip to your ATM, but deduct the amount from your total Flexible Money as though you wrote a check for it.

IT'S NO SURPRISE

Let's look closely at some examples of those unexpected, spontaneous, and emergency expenses—are they really unpredictable? Probably not as much as you think. It's more likely that you're not used to *thinking* of them and *planning* for them ahead of time. Even when expenses arise that are truly out of your control—doctor and vet bills, car repairs, traffic tickets, birthday presents, etc.—you can still plan the *payment* of these items without disrupting your current Spending Plan. Let's take a look.

Medical Expenses

Most doctors bill you for your visits instead of requiring full payment immediately, although this may be changing. When you schedule your appointment, think about whether you will work the payment into your Spending Plan for the month of the appointment (and pay with cash or check on the day of your visit) or the following month when you receive the bill. If the visit is an emergency and you can't fit the payment into this month's Spending Plan, you can pay for it the following month when you receive the bill.

If paying the full amount puts a strain on one month's Spending Plan, work out partial payments over a couple of months. If you know you'll need longer than three months to complete the full payment, call the doctor's billing office and let them know. Most offices appreciate the call and will not object to your payment plan, as long as you stick to it. Some medical and dental offices now accept credit cards, giving you yet another payment option for treatments that can't wait. Never hesitate to ask for a fee estimate before scheduling medical or dental treatment. Simply say, "Can you give me an estimate of the charges?"

Your Spending Plan is not intended to override your desire for the best medical treatment, but you might want to consider some of the many insurance plans available that require small payments and no paperwork. My favorite is one that uses preferred providers and all I pay is a fifteen-dollar copayment at the time of the visit. I use my Cash to Burn to cover this. There are HMOs available that require no payment. If you find the services meet your health-care needs, consider using these medical plans.

Planning a Trip?

The money for your major trip expenses (airline, hotel, and car rental) needs to be accumulated prior to the month of your trip (a benefit of starting a *Saving Habit*), or paid by your tax refund (a benefit of planning to receive a refund). However, the spending money for your trip can come from a combination of your Flexible Money and Cash to Burn for the weeks you'll be traveling. Remember, the Cash to Burn is money you would spend that week anyway.

Vet Expenses

If these are under $30, use your Cash to Burn. If they are over $30 and an emergency, ask the vet to bill you so you can pay in full the following month. When it's not possible for you to make the complete payment in one month, work out a payment plan spreading the total over a few months. For routine shots, ask for the price when you make the appointment and work it into your Spending Plan either from your Cash to Burn or the amount you've set aside for Flexible Money.

Traffic Tickets

You got caught! Certainly unpleasant, but you have at least thirty days to pay before the paperwork (and the police) catch up to you. Just put the ticket into your filing system (discussed in Chapter 14) for next month's Spending Plan. (Be aware of a new twist some local governments are using to raise money. It goes like this: An $11 parking ticket carries a $30 late fee if you don't pay it on time. That's right. Get that payment in!)

Birthday Presents

Birthdays may *sneak up* on you, but they certainly don't come as a surprise. They are the most consistent events I know of. Develop a system of listing birthdays by month. Look at the list at the beginning of each month, not only as part of creating your Spending Plan, but also to remind yourself to remember the arrival day of your loved ones.

Car Repairs

Some car repairs hit unexpectedly and you need to have the work done or you can't use your car. I recommend using your credit card in that situation. If you can pay the amount in full the following month, do it. If not, you may end up paying some interest. Pay as much of the balance as fast as you can until it's back to zero. If the repair isn't an emergency, schedule it for a month when you have the funds. Or, have it done the month before you have the funds, charge it, and pay your credit card in full the following month.

Hint: Consider getting an American Automobile Association card or the equivalent. They are designed to take the worry and some of the expense out of auto emergencies. If you break down unexpectedly, AAA makes sure you and your car are taken to a shop where you can calmly decide how you're going to handle the rest of the situation.

THE 10% SOLUTION

On your Master Spending Plan allow at *least* 10% of your monthly take-home income for Flexible Money to cover unknowns. Start with 10% and see how it works during the first six months you use your Spending Plan. The more activity, possessions, and people in your life, the more you will have spending surprises. Think about it: If you have two cars needing work you have twice as many auto maintenance bills. Nine cats needing to go to the vet will bring more vet bills, emergency and nonemergency, than one cat. Likewise, a family of five has more surprise spending requirements than a family of two. Start with 10% and adjust it up or down after you've worked with it for a while.

EXTRA MONEY? WHERE?

Right now you may be thinking something like this, "*Extra* money, I'm lucky just to cover my bills with the money I make. I've never had the luxury of extra money to spend!" This is a natural response with two possible causes: Either your past spending was not directed toward anything specific so the extra money slipped through your fingers, or you may not have enough income, which your Master Spending Plan will reveal.

For both situations, planning your spending is the answer. If you have enough money now, *plan* your spending so you acquire the items you want. If you need more income, use your Master Spending Plan to identify the right amount. With your total expenses listed in one place, calculate exactly how much more income you will need to have enough Flexible Money. Focusing on this number, devise ways to bring the extra income into your life. Discovering the facts about your situation is the first step. Doing something about it follows naturally.

Bella computes 10% of $1,500, her average monthly take-home pay, to come up with $150 for her Flexible Money. Bella thinks this will buy her plenty of choice new clothes every month from the local outlet mall, especially glittery nightclub outfits for her destiny as a singer. Not bad. With this Flexible Money she'll be in clothes heaven forever!

Bella, other expenses *will* come up. *All* of this money won't always be available for clothes every month. Remember to be flexible!

SUMMARY

Your Flexible Money covers emergencies, desires, and spontaneous spending. On your Master Spending Plan your Flexible Money is simply listed as 10% of your monthly income. On your Actual Spending Plan, you'll identify specific expenses as they come up, leaving some money available for last-minute spending opportunities. What you buy with your Flexible Money is up to you—you set your own priorities!

TAKE ACTION

- Start a Want List. Write down everything you want to buy as money becomes available. Keep the Want List in your Spending Plan binder. Whenever friends or relatives ask you what you want for your birthday or Christmas, you know where to look!

- Make a list of all the friends and relatives to remember with gifts on their special days. Organize this list by month and keep it in your Spending Plan binder.

SPENDING PLAN for Bella Femme

Month/Yr _____Master_____ End Date _____ No./Weeks _____4_____

INCOME			Plan	Actual	Diff.
Net Pay	Date	Amount			
		750			
		750	1,500		
Other					
Bottom Line —Last Month Surplus					
TOTAL INCOME			1,500		

EXPENSES		Plan	Actual	Diff.
Bottom Line - Last Month Negative				
Checks				
	House Payment	630		
	Car Payment	80		
	Donations	50		
	Phone	60		
	Utilities	25		
	Health Club	20		
	Hair & Beauty	30		
	CD Club	15		
	Voice	40		
Total Checks		950		
Cash $ __100__ x __4__ dollars weeks		400		
Flexible Money _____		*150*		
Total Flexible Money		*150*		
Credit Card Freedom				
_____				
_____				
_____				
Total Credit Card Freedom				
Start Saving Now! YES!				
TOTAL EXPENSES				

BOTTOM LINE	Plan	Actual	Diff.
(Income minus expenses)			

Chapter Seven

Get Your Credit Cards Under Control

> *I used to believe that if you were to go broke,*
> *meaning you ran out of money, that was it—*
> *you were broke, that was it! You know what I*
> *found out? You can whistle right on by zero.*
> *Zero is not the end.*
>
> —Anthony Robbins

Perhaps some of the most discouraging pieces of mail you receive are those #/@*#@*! credit card bills. Long after the thrill of the purchase is gone, these nasty notices show up to remind you your money is not your own. Wouldn't it be nice *not* to get credit cards bills ever again? What would life look like if you no longer had to relive the buying experience by paying for it when the credit card bill shows up?

ABSOLUTELY OBSOLETE

Many people got hooked on credit cards believing they didn't really pay for something if they just charged it. For a while, our government eased the pain by allowing tax deductions for interest payments, but those days are gone. Once upon a time, some financial sages recommended charging purchases to help your financial situation by postponing the payment thirty days or more. This let your payment money collect interest for you during that period. Look carefully at the assumptions behind this theory: (1) you *have* the money earning all that interest, (2) it *is* earning interest and not sitting idly in a non-interest checking account, and (3) you *pay* the bill before it starts charging you interest. Even if you follow those guidelines, charging gives you a boost *only* in the first month, since thereafter you shell out a regular monthly payment to pay the credit card bill. Soon, you're back where you started!

YOUR FINANCIAL FRIENDS

Credit cards are powerful tools offering two advantages necessary for financial health. First, they give you purchasing and payment convenience, and second they provide credit for emergencies. The difference between having a credit card that *helps* you and a credit card that *hurts* you, is *how you use it.* One financial expert describes credit cards as a source of help in small doses, a loss of freedom in large doses. The *Money Without Madness System* works best with the shifting power a credit card gives you, so don't get the scissors out yet.

CONVENIENCE

I use my credit card every month without fail. I make phone purchases for flowers, airline tickets, concert tickets, and some mail-order items. I may use it when I spontaneously decide to pick up a restaurant tab and don't have enough cash in my wallet (many restaurants don't accept checks). It is especially convenient for large payments such as car repairs and tuition. Over the last year, I've charged two to three items a month on my card simply for convenience, or to *shift* the payment for an emergency into the next month. By limiting my use of the credit card to emergency situations and purchases not possible to pay by check, my credit card balance stays reasonably low. On occasions when it gets too high, I feel it in the Spending Plan for the next month (ouch!) and cut back to emergency charges only.

GIVE ME CREDIT

The second advantage of a credit card is to provide an emergency line of credit if you lose your income. Think of it as insurance; you pay a small annual fee to reduce your risk. You hope never to lose your job and need to use this money, but it's a good idea to prepare while you *are* employed and get the highest limits you can. Having high limits does *not* obligate you to use the full credit available to you, does *not* cost you any more (unless you use it), and may come in handy at a critical time. (*Note*: People with credit card control problems may wisely choose to postpone this step.)

You obtain high credit limits by consistently using your credit card and showing good payment history. You need to *ask* for increases though, as they may not come automatically. Do this after you get a salary raise and have made a number of purchases recently with your card. If you are taking a trip, put the major expenses on your card, pay it off, then request an increase. It's probably *not* a good idea to call while the charges are still on your card because the credit card company may mistakenly think you're in trouble and can't pay your balance. Also, don't wait until *after* you are unemployed to ask for the increases because your steady paycheck plays a role in the company's evaluation of you as creditworthy.

THE RIGHT CARD(S)

Select a card that is accepted wherever you need to make a convenience charge. This comes down to one of the major *bank credit cards*. Take your pick. You may want to shop around, or just keep the one you already have. Try to find a card that requires only a small annual fee or none at all. A word on interest—the card I use carries an outrageous interest rate, as many do. I keep it because the high rate provides an incentive to me to always make my payment *in full* and *on time*. It would be pretty expensive for me to break the habit of making full payment, which is precisely the idea. You decide if this is comfortable for you.

What is the difference between a charge card and a credit card? A charge card requires you to *pay the balance in full* when you receive the bill. A credit card requires you to *pay a minimum amount* and lets the remainder be paid off over a period of time. A *credit* card is the one you want, since it provides the emergency credit we discussed earlier.

At most, you need two credit cards. There is a possibility you may shop at a store that takes one credit card but not another, and you want flexibility. You can build more emergency credit with two cards instead of one. If you consistently charge business expenses, it is easier to have two cards and use one for business expenses only.

Some people carry a gas charge card to cover road emergencies. If you are in the habit of charging all your gas and paying for it in full on a monthly basis, it's okay to continue, as long as you include the typical monthly amount with your other bills under the CHECKS category.

FAITH, HOPE, AND CHARGING

Department store cards are another story. If you use these cards, you are probably one of two kinds of people. Either you are a frequent shopper and use the cards for the convenience of receiving one monthly bill you gladly pay in full, or you are living on the edge and use the cards when you want to buy something and don't have the money yet. You hope (and pray) that by charging it, you postpone the payment problem and some money will show up. You know who you are! Person Number One, keep your cards. Person Number Two, read on. . . .

THE GHOST OF PURCHASES PAST

One of the three key money habits to add to your life is to *Gain Credit Card Freedom*. The first step required is to eliminate credit card debt—forever. Credit card debt is unlike other debt because it is optional. Avoidable. Unnecessary. It may be difficult for the average person to obtain a house, car, and sometimes a college degree without funding the payments with debt. It is not difficult to buy a flatware set at your department store without charging it. Department stores take cash and checks as well. When you pay for everyday purchases with current money, the past does not haunt you. When you pay with a credit card, the ghost of your past purchases visits frequently to rattle your bucks.

BREAK THE CYCLE

Ultimately *you will pay*. If you charge now, you will pay later. When later comes, you pay for things you no longer remember, leaving you less money for the things you *know* you want *right now*. Which leaves you with only two choices: don't buy it (hard, I know), or charge it (even worse). Charging causes charging. It's difficult to get out of the cycle. Once you do get out, it's easy to stay out by spending *today's* money for *today's* purchases instead of borrowing tomorrow's money by charging. Just look at your Spending Plan after you total the CREDIT CARD FREEDOM section and ask yourself if it would be nice to have that money to spend right now instead of paying off your credit card bill. Would it? Of course it would! Keep this as motivation to *eliminate credit card debt forever!*

DOWN, CARDS, DOWN!

When your credit cards are at their limits, you have nowhere to go for emergency money. If disaster strikes your car's transmission, you'll be taking the ankle express to work and play.

No one should be without credit for emergencies. It's not kind to yourself, and it is not wise planning for a sound financial future. Pay your credit card balances down, and keep them down.

DO IT

On your Master Spending Plan, put amounts for the minimum payments on all your credit cards, charge cards, and department store cards under the category labeled CREDIT CARD FREEDOM. List them separately so you can match the payments to the planned amount. Later, you can determine whether or not you want to pay more aggressively to reduce your debt faster. Your Actual Spending Plan will show you how much money is available to do that. If you currently have your credit cards under control and pay your balances in full every month, put an *average* balance amount in the appropriate blank.

Your Spending Plan lists your credit card debt separately so you can work this section to zero over time. Showing it separately also gives you an exact total of how much current money is paying for your *past purchases*, or charges. It's helpful to see if this is a significant portion of your income. After your credit card debt is gone, you can use that money for other wonderful purposes—more spending *now* or to increase savings.

Our friend Bella has two credit cards and a charge card at the department store where she works. She lists the minimum payment of each credit card ($25 and $40) and the full balance of her department store card ($120). The total comes to $185. Curious, she adds the total amounts owed on all her cards and comes up with $1,542. This is more than she thought it would be! Bella didn't realize how much she'd charged. This surprise is a little unsettling. How is she going to pay $1,542 of credit card debt?

SPENDING PLAN for Bella Femme

Month/Yr __Master__ End Date _____ No./Weeks __4__

INCOME			Plan	Actual	Diff.
Net Pay	Date	Amount			
		750			
		750	1,500		
Other					
Bottom Line —Last Month Surplus					
TOTAL INCOME			1,500		

EXPENSES		Plan	Actual	Diff.
Bottom Line-Last Month Negative				
Checks				
	House Payment	630		
	Car Payment	80		
	Donations	50		
	Phone	60		
	Utilities	25		
	Health Club	20		
	Hair & Beauty	30		
	CD Club	15		
	Voice	40		
Total Checks		950		
Cash $__100__ x __4__ dollars weeks		400		
Flexible Money _____		150		
Total Flexible Money		150		
Credit Card Freedom				
	Master Card	25		
	VISA	40		
	Department Store	120		
Total Credit Card Freedom		185		
Start Saving Now! YES!				
TOTAL EXPENSES				

BOTTOM LINE	Plan	Actual	Diff.
(Income minus expenses)			

Don't be discouraged, Bella. A balance of $1,542 may seem high, but you'll be able to pay it down. Keep going and you'll figure out how. You're better off knowing what you owe so you can take action to reduce it. A lot of people aren't even willing to take an honest look at their money like you just did. You're doing great with this. Some folks might even stop right now if they didn't like what they just saw.

You're not going to stop now are you Bella?

To be honest, Bella would rather not think about it anymore. She's going to take a break and join us again after practicing a few new voice pieces. That'll lift her spirits.

SUMMARY

Credit Card Freedom is more than just paying off your credit card debt. Use your cards for shifting payments, getting quick credit in emergencies, and making certain purchases conveniently. As long as you pay your credit card balance in full each month, your cards are working for you. If not, you're working for your cards. Don't let that continue. One of the ways you keep your money from escaping is by limiting your charges. If you use a credit card infrequently, you already know the beauty of it. If you don't, make it a goal to pay off and close all but two major bank credit cards and see how much simpler your money management becomes.

TAKE ACTION

- Total all your credit card debt. How many months will it take to pay it off if you make the minimum payments and don't charge any more? How long if you double each minimum payment?

- Think about how you would buy differently if credit cards did not exist. Be creative. Try some of these ideas over the next few months instead of charging.

Chapter Eight

Build a Savings Plan

> *Better to have and not need, than need and not have.*
>
> —Czechoslovakian grandmother

"Don't all parents teach their children about money?" Sophia directs this question to me as she shampoos Winnie's hair. Winnie is president and owner of a public relations company and we met here because her schedule was filled. Sophia and her partner own the salon. Sophia explains, "My father used to come home and show us whatever money he made, and together the family would decide what to buy—after half of it went in the bank. Is this a cultural difference?" Sophia's parents are from Croatia. She continues, "When I was young my parents always saved half of what they earned and it's a habit I've kept ever since." She's got my attention like a drop in interest rates. Half? *Half!* I've never heard of anyone saving *half* of what they make. Is Sophia exceptional, or am I in the dark about saving money?

Forty minutes later, Sophia puts the final touches on Winnie's new "do" and continues the chitchat, "Oh Winnie, we bought a new house." Unsurprised, Winnie laughs, "The land baroness!" Sophia already owns several pieces of property in

Silicon Valley. As Sophia quietly reveals the shrewd details of her latest investment, I focus on her wealth strategy—save half of what you earn and invest it. But *how* is still a mystery to me. Perhaps Sophia's right, maybe this is a cultural difference.

THE CRÈME DE LA CRÈME

Saving money is your ultimate financial goal. Saving money means you're taking in more than you're spending every month. It is the equivalent of profit in a healthy business. Once you've saved money, you have a splendid selection of choices: large purchases (furniture, travel, recreation equipment); a Safety Fund for emergencies; down payments on cars, houses, boats, or airplanes; paying off remaining credit card debt; retirement planning; college tuition for the toddlers; and an exciting variety of investments.

What's most important to you? What do you want to save for? How do you want your savings to add to your life? Your savings buy the things that are above and beyond the everyday expenses of your life. Saved money buys you *more* than you can buy with paycheck-to-paycheck money. Saved money gets you ahead. Without savings it is difficult to pay for more than the monthly expenses already listed on your Spending Plan. Your ultimate goal is to **Start Saving Now** and make it a lifetime habit. With a steady amount of money always building your savings, you are free to spend it, invest it, and use it for any of your financial goals.

WHICH CRÈME FIRST?

Some balancing is necessary. If you have little or no furniture, you may balance your first savings goals between saving for major purchases you need now and building a Safety Fund for emergencies. Once you have the Safety Fund established, leave it there. Don't deplete it. Like it says on those exit signs, it is to "Use Only in Emergency."

When you've conquered these two priorities, move on. The next balancing act might be between directing your savings toward the down payment on a house and starting a retirement fund. You can tackle both at once, or save the down payment first then save for retirement. It's up to you, your age, and your priorities in life. Just don't forget the retirement planning part. This topic can fill another book, but if you start by learning the benefits of compounding, saving money in an Individual Retirement Account (IRA) or 401K plan, and thinking about your golden years, you're on your way!

After these priorities are satisfied, you have more freedom as your savings continue to build—a vacation home in Tahiti, a long sabbatical in the south of France, a multitude of portfolio options, a forty-foot schooner, charm school for the youngsters, a lipstick red Lamborghini. You won't run out of ideas to enjoy this money!

SAFETY FUND, SAFETY NET

It's easy to determine the amount of money you want in your Safety Fund by reviewing your most recent Spending Plans. Count on *all* your expenses continuing if you are liberated from your job. Once you get used to a certain level of spending, it can be difficult to suddenly cut back. With other changes resulting from the absence of a steady paycheck, you won't need added pressure by suddenly trying to lower your spending. Calculate a reasonable average for your monthly spending and multiply by the number of months you expect it would take you to find another *satisfactory* job. This might range anywhere from three to nine months depending on the type of work you do and the area where you live. If you think it might take longer, plan to cover more time off. Do *not* underestimate the amount of time you need to provide your own support—it is better to plan for more than not enough.

PICTURE THAT GOAL!

Some people like to identify goals for saving money. You may tell yourself, "I'm buying my vacation in advance" when you write the check for your savings, or "Here's a check toward retirement at age thirty-five." By doing this, you associate the money you're socking away with specific goals that are important to you rather than merely putting it into a bank where you're not sure what good it will do (except grow).

When you do this, remember to *continue* the **Saving Habit** after the vacation is taken, the house is purchased, etc. It really is a lifetime habit to keep rather than a temporary measure to use for just one item. It's okay to spend saved money as long as more money is *always coming in*. If you lose the habit because you see nothing to save for, it will be hard to pick it up again when your life changes and you suddenly need some savings.

HOW MUCH?

I recommend building up to a habit of saving at *least* 10% of your take-home income. This means if your monthly take-home pay is $1,750, you'll save $175 each month and have $2,100 at the end of the first year. Remember, your savings payment increases when your income increases, so don't forget to calculate a new amount when you receive a raise.

After you've reached the 10% level, you may decide you want to increase the amount of money you save. For some people, 10% is not enough to cover their requirements for getting ahead. Calculate how much money you'll save over a three-year period at 10% each year. Compare that to your dreams. Will it get you there? What amount will? Perhaps you want to save half your money like Sophia, and make impressive investment strides!

Use your Master Spending Plan to see how much money is available for extra saving. Don't be overly aggressive and lower your Cash to Burn and Flexible Money beyond reasonable amounts. It won't be long before you'll tire of this, and you may overreact by giving up the **Saving Habit** altogether. Your Spending Plan works best with gradual, permanent changes instead of sudden, overzealous jumps.

STASH YOUR CASH

Two steps make it easier to start your **Saving Habit**. First, be sure to set up a separate savings account. Do not mix your saved money with your checking account money. It is too easy to spend. Second, take advantage of any automatic payment program your company offers to split-deposit your paycheck between your checking and savings accounts. This service allows you to determine how much of each check goes into your savings account and have it deposited automatically. You never get a chance to see it or spend it. If this makes you nervous about overdrawing, then skip it and write yourself a check at the end of the month from checking to savings. Later, you can automate.

You don't have to start your **Saving Habit** at the full 10%. Instead, you can build up to that level of savings over time. One of the best times to start saving, or to move to a higher savings percentage, is when you receive a raise. By putting a portion of the additional money directly toward your savings right away, you avoid getting used to living on the higher amount, and then having to cut back to build your **Saving Habit.**

DO IT

Calculate a monthly savings payment based on the goal of 10% of your take-home monthly salary. (To keep this calculation simple, divide your annual take-home salary first by twelve then by ten to calculate the payment instead of breaking it down to 10% of a weekly salary.) Put this number on your

Spending Plan in the box across from the line titled START SAV-
ING NOW! Starting with 10% now is an optimistic move and you
may soon revise this number downward to a more realistic figure, but it's a good idea to see what you're working toward.

If your income fluctuates, use your monthly income *estimate*
to calculate a savings amount. Keep your monthly savings
constant even when your income goes up and down and
you'll keep your planning simple. However, adjust it occasionally when you see a reliable new trend developing in your
income pattern.

Bella expects to earn approximately $1,500 each month and
wants to save 10% of that. Dividing $1,500 by ten, she calcu-
lates a savings amount of $150 and puts this on her Spending
Plan. Being single and unattached, she dreams of a Club Med
week in Cancun. She figures she'll need the vacation after paying off all her credit cards!

Bella, since you don't have any savings yet, don't you want to
think about emergencies and set up a Safety Fund first?

Not really. Bella's more interested in relaxing under the
Mexican sun right now. She figures there's plenty of time for
Safety Funds after Cancun.

Okay Bella, whatever jump starts your ***Saving Habit*** is fine
with me. After all, it's your choice!

SUMMARY

Saving money every month is a sign of financial health and a
mechanism for your money to bring you enjoyment beyond
day-to-day living. With money in savings, you are free to
decide how to use it. Without money in savings, you have
fewer choices and a financially restricted lifestyle. With an
entrenched ***Saving Habit*** you are free to spend your savings
as you want to, confident it will be replenished over time. Start
a ***Saving Habit*** and *get addicted!*

SPENDING PLAN for Bella Femme

Month/Yr __Master__ End Date _____ No./Weeks __4__

INCOME			Plan	Actual	Diff.
Net Pay	Date	Amount 750			
		750	1,500		
Other					
Bottom Line —Last Month Surplus					
TOTAL INCOME			1,500		

EXPENSES	Plan	Actual	Diff.
Bottom Line -Last Month Negative			
Checks			
House Payment	630		
Car Payment	80		
Donations	50		
Phone	60		
Utilities	25		
Health Club	20		
Hair & Beauty	30		
CD Club	15		
Voice	40		
Total Checks	950		
Cash $ __100__ x __4__ dollars weeks	400		
Flexible Money _____	150		
Total Flexible Money	150		
Credit Card Freedom			
Master Card	25		
VISA	40		
Department Store	120		
Total Credit Card Freedom	185		
Start Saving Now! YES!	*150*		
TOTAL EXPENSES			

BOTTOM LINE	Plan	Actual	Diff.
(Income minus expenses)			

TAKE ACTION

- Open a savings account.

- Calculate how much you'd like to set aside for your Safety Fund.

- Sign up for automatic deposit of your paycheck, even if it all goes to checking.

- Imagine you already have one year of living expenses saved and all your credit cards paid off. How does it feel? What would you do differently?

- Buy a basic investment book and read about compounding, IRAs, and 401K plans.

Chapter Nine

Design a Master Spending Plan

When money talks the truth is silent.

—Russian proverb

Go ahead and total your Master Spending Plan. All the numbers are in place. Add the boxes with light borders around them (TOTAL CHECKS, CASH, etc.) together and put the total in the heavily bordered box toward the bottom called TOTAL EXPENSES. Use a calculator and do your math twice, so you're sure the numbers you're working with are correct. Subtract TOTAL EXPENSES from TOTAL INCOME and put the number in the box called BOTTOM LINE. Is it positive, negative, or close to zero? If it's negative, put parentheses ( ) or brackets < > around it.

How does Bella's Master Spending Plan look? She adds her expenses to come to a total of $1,835. It seems too high, so she adds it again using her calculator. Yes, $1,835 is the right number. With Total Income of $1,500 and Total Expenses of $1,835, she shows a negative Bottom Line of $335. Another unsettling surprise! She quickly double checks her math again to make sure it's right. Yes, it is. If this is true, she won't even get by next month. There's no hope of paying down her

SPENDING PLAN for Bella Femme

Month/Yr ___Master___ End Date _____ No./Weeks ___4___

INCOME			Plan	Actual	Diff.
	Date	Amount			
Net Pay	_____	750			
	_____	750	1,500	_____	_____
Other		_____	_____	_____	
Bottom Line —Last Month Surplus			_____	_____	
TOTAL INCOME			1,500		

EXPENSES	Plan	Actual	Diff.
Bottom Line -Last Month Negative			
Checks			
House Payment	630	_____	
Car Payment	80	_____	
Donations	50	_____	
Phone	60	_____	
Utilities	25	_____	
Health Club	20	_____	
Hair & Beauty	30	_____	
CD Club	15		
Voice	40		
Total Checks	950		
Cash $___100___ x ___4___ dollars weeks	400		
Flexible Money _____	150	_____	
_____	_____	_____	
Total Flexible Money	150		
Credit Card Freedom			
Master Card	25	_____	
VISA	40	_____	
Department Store	120	_____	
Total Credit Card Freedom	185		
Start Saving Now! YES!	150		
TOTAL EXPENSES	1,835		

BOTTOM LINE	Plan	Actual	Diff.
(Income minus expenses)	335		

credit cards. What will she do? She's starting to feel nervous, unsure, she might even be . . . panicking!

DON'T PANIC!

Do you have a negative BOTTOM LINE? Don't panic. Remember, what you've just completed might be closer to the *ideal* plan for spending your money rather than a realistic plan that works right now. After all, you used a full 10% for your savings amount and you may not be able to start at that level. The idea of doing your Master Spending Plan first is to see how close you are to the ideal and then play with the numbers once they are on paper. Now you're ready to make changes to reflect what's realistic. Let's see how Bella changes her Master Spending Plan.

PLAYING ON PAPER

First, Bella eliminates her savings goal of $150, lowering her negative bottom line to $185. Reducing her weekly Cash to Burn to $80 gives her $80 more ($20 x 4) decreasing the negative total to $105—still unacceptable. Looking down the list of expenses, she finds Donations at $50 and reduces it to $20. The difference of $30 brings her total BOTTOM LINE to negative $75, a little better. The only categories left are FLEXIBLE MONEY and CREDIT CARD FREEDOM. Much as she'd like to spend $150 on clothes this month, she opts for putting $30 of it toward her negative BOTTOM LINE, keeping $120 for her wardrobe. Her BOTTOM LINE is now down to negative $45—something still has to give! The only category left is CREDIT CARD FREEDOM. Bella really wants to get rid of that credit card debt soon so she's reluctant to take any money out of this category. Still, she's left with negative $45 and has to make a change somewhere. Hmm.

SPENDING PLAN for Bella Femme

Month/Yr ___Master___ End Date _____ No./Weeks ___4___

INCOME			Plan	Revision #1	Diff.
	Date	Amount			
Net Pay	_____	750			
	_____	750	1,500	*1,500*	
Other			_____	_____	
Bottom Line —Last Month Surplus			_____	_____	
TOTAL INCOME			1,500	*1,500*	

EXPENSES	Plan	Actual	Diff.
Bottom Line -Last Month Negative			
Checks			
House Payment	630	*630*	
Car Payment	80	*80*	
Donations	50	*20*	
Phone	60	*60*	
Utilities	25	*25*	
Health Club	20	*20*	
Hair & Beauty	30	*30*	
CD Club	15	*15*	
Voice	40	*40*	
Total Checks	950	*920*	
Cash $___100___ x ___4___	400	*320*	
dollars weeks			
Flexible Money _____	150	*120*	
Total Flexible Money	150	*120*	
Credit Card Freedom			
Master Card	25	*25*	
VISA	40	*40*	
Department Store	120	*120*	
Total Credit Card Freedom	185	*185*	
Start Saving Now! YES!	150	*0*	
TOTAL EXPENSES	1,835	*1,545*	

BOTTOM LINE	Plan	Actual	Diff.
(Income minus expenses)	<335>	*45*	

NO, NO, NO . . .

While Bella mulls this over, let's go over some mistakes you want to avoid when squeezing money out of a Spending Plan. Some predictable mindsets appear when people get religious about money. These are often short-lived bursts that only use a lot of energy, burn people out, and discourage further progress. You'll have more success if you avoid the following tactics when developing your Spending Plan.

NO SURPRISES

It's tempting to convince yourself that there really won't be any surprises each month so your Flexible Money can be much lower. Yes, you can lower it a little and see how well that works for you. Ten percent is a guideline that may or may not be the right amount for you. If you decrease it, pay close attention to your comfort level during the next several months. If you find yourself sweating because the dog's shots are due, panicking when the right headlight on your car burns out, or cursing the dentist who tells you your back molar needs a crown, you may not be providing enough Flexible Money for surprises. These misfortunes are not singling you out—these are normal expenses. You don't need to be happy about them. You do need to provide enough Flexible Money to cover them.

NO DENIAL

Don't get so carried away with paying off your credit cards and saving money that you deny yourself Flexible Money for the things you'll want to buy spontaneously or from your Want List. You may be the kind of person who can truly eliminate all spending that's not totally necessary for absolute survival—but *why would you want to?* If you need to cut some expenses, use a balanced approach so it will last. If you don't keep balance in your spending, you may feel deprived during the month. Resentment has a sneaky way of building up and can quickly sabotage your progress. With a realistic plan including Flexible Money for fun each month, you know you can buy an item next month if you've used all your Flexible Money this month. No denial. Just a shift from now to next month.

If you are really motivated to use some of your Flexible Money to pay off your credit cards or to start saving, do it this way: Leave the money in your Flexible Money category. That way, it's available during the month if you need it. At the *end* of the month, put whatever amount remains toward the goal you want. By waiting until the end of the month, you use money that is *truly* extra, not *hopefully* extra.

NO STARVING

Don't go too skinny on your Cash to Burn either. Most of the items you pay for with this money are for your basic welfare (food, gas, drugstore, entertainment) and it isn't good to starve your well-being on a consistent basis. Your plan will backfire and fall apart if you're not realistic in this area as well.

NO FOOLING AROUND

On the other hand, there may be some give and take in your Cash to Burn. If you lower it, make sure you keep the amount constant each week. For example, suppose your Cash to Burn is $100, but you think you can really get by with just $90 a week instead. Since your ATM only gives out $20s you figure you'll get $100 one week and $80 the next, for an average of $90 a week. Yes, the math in this tactic works, but you've added complexity to the system that opens you up to errors. Don't fool yourself. Better to stick to $20 increments, or make out a check for $90 each week and cash it at the teller's window inside the bank.

NO KIDDING

Don't kid yourself about your numbers. Let's say you need some extra money from somewhere and you're looking at the amount you've put down for phone expense—$60. After thinking about this for a while, you convince yourself the phone bill really can be lowered to $25 because you'll stop calling your sister-in-law. Okay, maybe you won't *stop* calling her altogether; after all, she is thinking about quitting her job, so you want all the updates. Maybe you'll just *shorten* the phone calls. True, it's never happened yet, but you're sure you can do it.

Go ahead and make that change in phone time. *After* you see the results in your phone bill, change your Master Spending Plan. If your phone bills until now have averaged $60, then $60 is the correct number to use until that number comes down. If you use a lower number too soon, you are speculating and may inadvertently be building bad news into your Spending Plan. Better to keep the amount for your phone bill at $60, make all efforts to reduce the phone time to your sister-in-law, and see the good news when it comes in—a phone bill for $25 when you planned on $60. That's an extra $35-worth of good news!

NO GUESSING GAMES

Take the guesswork out of your money predictions. Use real numbers in your Spending Plan and use your motivation to improve on your Plan. You may decide to find a moonlighting job to pay your credit cards off faster. Great. Don't put an estimate on your Spending Plan until you have the job and know how much you'll get from it. Until you see a paycheck, make sure your Spending Plan works without that money. You can always make an extra credit card payment when you total everything up at the end of the month and find a surplus from the moonlighting check. Build your Spending Plan so it's likely to be bombarded with good news instead of bad.

BACK TO BELLA

So Bella, how's your negative Bottom Line of $45? What ideas have you come up with?

Bella decides there's only one tactic that's realistic this month. She'll take $45 off her $120 department store bill, pay $75 instead of the full amount, and face the consequences. She's supposed to pay the full amount since it's a *charge* card, not a credit card, but she's willing to take her chances on this one. Perhaps they won't catch it right away. If she doesn't add any more charges, she knows she'll pay the full balance next month, then close the account. With $120 left in Flexible Money each month, she should be able to pay for any new clothes with checks instead of by charging them, if she really tries.

Bella puts her revised Master Spending Plan numbers in the column next to the original one and rechecks the math to make sure there are no mistakes. She looks over the items that changed and thinks about what she'd like to work toward in future months. After next month, her total payment for CREDIT CARD FREEDOM will be only $110, and the month after that it will be down to $65—if she stops charging now. That'll free up another $30 next month and $45 more the following month. After the next three months, she'll have $75 ($30 plus $45) more to put wherever she wants. What'll it be?

She may need to bring her Cash to Burn back up to $100 a week. After testing it this month she'll have a better idea of what's practical. She also wants to start a *Saving Habit* (Cancun, watch out). Then again, the interest she's paying on her credit card total of $1,500 is frightening (almost $25 a month), so she'd like to get rid of that. If she makes only the minimum payments every month, she'll pay so much money in interest it will take her years get to Cancun.

Decisions, decisions. Bella vows to lay off the credit cards and pulls out another blank Spending Plan to do some "What If?" scenarios. She makes the following changes:

Income—up to $1,700 a month

Cash to Burn—up to $100 a week ($400 monthly)

Flexible Money—up to $170 (10% of $1,700)

This gives her $70 more a month, in addition to the extra $75 she frees up after paying her department store account. If she reaches this level of income in three months, she'll add all of it to the $65 in monthly payments toward her credit card balances to pay a total of $210 every month. This will bring her balances to zero much faster. In three months she'll owe roughly $1,350. Bella calculates it'll take her about seven months to pay it all off ($1,350 divided by her new $210 monthly payment). That's just over half a year! After that she'll have no debt payments and a comfortable level of Cash to Burn and Flexible Money. She'll put the $210 toward her savings goal and get set for Cancun!

Good job juggling the numbers, Bella. You're off to a great start—now how do we turn your great start into a Cancun fiesta? Let's put your Spending Plan to work as a monthly guide for actual dollars-out-the-door, and there'll be no stopping you! Final details coming right up.

HAPPY DAYS

Congratulations if your Bottom Line is a positive number or close to zero when you create your Master Spending Plan. Follow the *Money Without Madness System* for a few months to make sure you haven't forgotten any expenses before making outgoing plans for that money. After that, happy spending!

SPENDING PLAN *for Bella Femme*

Month/Yr ___Master___ End Date _____ No./Weeks ___4___

INCOME			Plan	Revision #2	Diff.
	Date	Amount			
Net Pay	_____	750			
	_____	750	1,500	1,500	
Other					
Bottom Line —Last Month Surplus					
TOTAL INCOME			1,500	1,500	

EXPENSES		Plan	Actual	Diff.
Bottom Line -Last Month Negative				
Checks				
	House Payment	630	630	
	Car Payment	80	80	
	Donations	50	20	
	Phone	60	60	
	Utilities	25	25	
	Health Club	20	20	
	Hair & Beauty	30	30	
	CD Club	15	15	
	Voice	40	40	
Total Checks		950	920	
Cash $__100__ x __4__ dollars weeks		400	320	
Flexible Money _____		150	120	
Total Flexible Money		150	120	
Credit Card Freedom				
Master Card		25	25	
VISA		40	40	
Department Store		120	*75*	
Total Credit Card Freedom		185	*140*	
Start Saving Now! YES!		150	*0*	
TOTAL EXPENSES		1,835	*1,500*	

BOTTOM LINE	Plan	Actual	Diff.
(Income minus expenses)	<335>	0	

SUMMARY

Much of the information you just used for your Master Spending Plan remains the same for your Actual Spending Plan. After playing with the numbers to get your Bottom Line to zero, you have an excellent start for next month's Actual Spending Plan. Make a new Master Spending Plan whenever you want to see how major changes will affect your money situation. Your Master Spending Plan helps you *plan* for success with your money instead of *hoping* for it.

TAKE ACTION

- If you have a positive Bottom Line, think about what you'd like to do with the extra money.

- If your Bottom Line is negative, think about what changes will bring it closer to zero, and eventually to a positive number.

- Do some "What If?" scenarios with your Spending Plan. What if your income were higher? What if you had no debt payments?

Chapter Ten

Putting Your Spending Plan to Work

Your future results not from tomorrow's decisions, but from the results of today's decisions.

—Expert on business management

As your Master Spending Plan allows you to see one month's *average* spending, your Actual Spending Plan allows you to see the details of a particular month's *actual* spending. Once you've done a Master Spending Plan, the Actual Spending Plan is easy because you use the same form.

LOOKING FORWARD

At the beginning of each month, you'll make a new Spending Plan with current information. This is when you strategize, play with the numbers, manipulate your money on paper, and see what options you have. If you're making excellent progress toward your goals, you'll see it clearly in black and white. If you're not satisfied with your progress, this is your opportunity to recommit to your financial goals and come up with a plan of action to move forward. Your Actual Spending Plan is your tool to turn theory and ideas into reality.

LOOKING BACK

At the end of each month, you'll put the *actual* amounts you spent into the Spending Plan you created in the ACTUAL column and compare them to your planned amounts. This is important for several reasons: (1) it provides necessary feedback (either positive or negative, but always accurate); (2) it highlights important spending information to use in making next month's Spending Plan; (3) it gives you motivation to improve next month if you need to; and (4) it gives you an exact number (your Bottom Line) to carry forward to next month's Spending Plan to automatically correct any over- or underspending.

GETTING STARTED

Let's create your first Spending Plan for the upcoming month. The only change from the Master Spending Plan you've already completed is to put exact numbers in place of the estimates you used. On your Master Spending Plan you estimated how much your phone bill costs you each month. On your Actual Spending Plan you use the exact amount because you have the bill in front of you. Easy. On your Master Spending Plan you allowed 10% of your income for Flexible Money. When you prepare your Actual Spending Plan, you include the specific amounts of one-time expenses known to you at the beginning of the month. These go in the FLEXIBLE MONEY category. With exact dollar amounts you see exactly how much Flexible Money is available to you this month, how much debt you can pay off, and how much you can put into savings.

On your new Spending Plan, list each item in the column titled PLAN according to what you now know it to be. List your income for the month ahead of you. Gather all the paperwork for your bills and list each amount on the appropriate line. Cash is easy. Enter the number of weeks in the month (either four or five) and multiply that number by your weekly Cash to Burn. Done.

Move to these two categories next: CREDIT CARD FREEDOM and START SAVING NOW! Put down what you *must* pay on your debts and what you'd *like* to pay this month toward your **Saving Habit.** If you haven't been using a pencil, switch to one now. These are first guess numbers. When all is said and done, you may need to do some juggling between these two categories and your FLEXIBLE MONEY.

Next, think of any items coming up this month that are one-time expenses (school supplies, gifts, workshop fees, show tickets, kitchen paint, etc.). Write those in the blanks under FLEXIBLE MONEY. Look over last month's bills to remind yourself of anything that isn't paid off such as a dentist or vet bill. Look through the papers in your bill file for notices of money due, such as an auto registration fee or professional dues. Check your Want List for those goodies you've waited for long enough. Check your calendar for any appointments that carry a price tag (massage, hair salon, palm reading, etc.). Be sure to leave some money for spontaneous spending during the month (rollerblading with your favorite child, new aerobics gear, etc.).

GOOD NEWS

Calculate this month's planned BOTTOM LINE by totaling your INCOME and subtracting your EXPENSES. Is anything left over? If you have extra money, great. Use it to pay off more debt, add it to your savings, or for more Flexible Money. Wherever you decide to spend it, put the additional money in that category now and recalculate your BOTTOM LINE. When your new Spending Plan is done, the BOTTOM LINE is close to zero. Write down the amount of Flexible Money you want to spend this month on a Post-it™ note. Attach the note to your check register and keep track of what you spend, making sure not to exceed the total.

BAD NEWS

Is your BOTTOM LINE negative? Do your TOTAL EXPENSES exceed your TOTAL INCOME already? Here's where the juggling comes in. What expenses can you partially pay or push off until next month? Which expenses are flexible and which are not? Play with the numbers until you have a BOTTOM LINE close to zero. Keep your Cash to Burn amount constant or you'll add confusion to your spending habits. Experiment with some of your payments. What happens if you pay half your phone bill this month, reduce your long distance calls, and pay the remainder next month? Can you take action to lower any of your bills on a long-term basis? Can any of the purchases made with Flexible Money be postponed? Be careful to keep some money for surprises and spontaneous spending or your Spending Plan isn't realistic. You're not done until your BOTTOM LINE is zero. Keep working with your Spending Plan until you get it there.

CARRY ON

Now the fun starts. Throughout the month, use your Spending Plan to guide your buying. Remember the three escapes routes: cash, check, and charge. Get your weekly Cash-to-Burn and spend it however you like. Use checks (or a debit card) for your Flexible Spending, including spontaneous buys, and track this total. Limit your credit card purchases whenever you can. Notice when the plan works for you. When it doesn't work, make adjustments. It's your tool. Before you know it, one fast month is over, and it's time to . . .

REVIEW THE PAST

How does your actual spending for the last month compare to what you planned to spend? To find out, list all the checkbook entries that apply to the past month on your past month's Spending Plan in the column labeled ACTUAL. As you do this, mark the entry in your checkbook with the first letter of the month it belongs to. Use a different colored pen for each month. For instance, all items in April's Spending Plan may be marked with a red A for April. Next month use a green M to indicate those that are included in May's Spending Plan. As you go through your checkbook, all unmarked new items are entered on the Spending Plan for the month completed unless they are recent and apply to the upcoming month.

When you have several entries that apply to one line on your Spending Plan (Cash to Burn for example), total them in the margin of your Spending Plan, marking them as you list them. Then enter the total on the appropriate line on your Spending Plan. (Don't forget to use your calculator and add them twice.)

Once you've entered all the numbers on your Spending Plan, total each category. Add your TOTAL EXPENSES and deduct this from your TOTAL INCOME. This is your *actual* BOTTOM LINE for the month. If the number is negative, it means you overspent, if it is positive, you spent *less* money than you took in. To keep things straight, always put a negative Bottom Line number in parentheses ( ) or brackets < >.

IS IT RIGHT?

How do you know you've done everything correctly? Check the BOTTOM LINE total to your checkbook total. The BOTTOM LINE of your Spending Plan in the ACTUAL column represents the amount of money in your checkbook *at that time.* If you have *not* made any entries since then, this will be the same number as the total now in your checkbook.

More likely, you've made entries belonging to the upcoming month, for instance, an ATM withdrawal or receipt of a paycheck. You need to *adjust* the ending total in your checkbook, on a separate piece of paper, to get a number that excludes those items. This is an easy step and takes only two minutes.

Simply back out those entries. To back out an entry, start with the ending total in your checkbook, *subtract* any deposits that do not belong to last month, and *add* any checks or withdrawals that are excluded from the month you're working on. These are items that do *not* have a colored letter next to them. This gives you the correct number to compare to your BOTTOM LINE. (*Hint*: To help you remember how to back out entries, think of it as backward. Normally you *add* deposits, but in this case you do the backward, or opposite, action—you *subtract* them. Likewise with checks and withdrawals.)

UH-OH

If you don't come to the same number, you need to recheck a few things. How much is the difference? Is this a familiar number? Have you missed transferring it from your checkbook to your Spending Plan? Is it an even number, like an even $10? If so, it's likely you made a math error, so recheck your math. Make sure you entered all your checkbook amounts correctly on your Spending Plan. Make sure you backed out the correct numbers in your final adjustment step. Have you entered all deposits correctly as income on your Spending Plan, and checks and withdrawals as expenses? If the difference is not large (between $5 to $10), skip it and move on.

DIFFERENCES—FAVORABLE AND OTHERWISE

How well did you manage your spending last month? Is your BOTTOM LINE better than planned, right on target, or a little off? *More* than a little off? If it is, look at each category and compare the total you *actually* spent with the total you *planned* to spend. Use the boxes in the column called DIFFERENCE to calculate the differences between your planned total and your actual total by category. If the difference is favorable (you spent *less* than you planned or received *more* income) put an F or a plus sign next to it. If it's unfavorable mark it with a

U or a minus sign. This helps you see at a glance where you need to focus your efforts next month to meet your Spending Plan.

ROLLING FORWARD

What do you do with a surplus or deficit Bottom Line? You carry it into next month's Spending Plan. If the amount is negative from overspending, it reduces the amount of money you have to spend next month, so list it under EXPENSES in the box next to BOTTOM LINE—LAST MONTH NEGATIVE. In effect, you've borrowed from next month's money by spending money you didn't have last month. If the opposite occurred and you spent *less* than your income last month, you carry forward a surplus and have *more* to spend next month (happy days!). In this case, list it in the INCOME section on the line next to BOTTOM LINE—LAST MONTH SURPLUS since it increases the money you can use next month.

REFLECT ON IT

It's possible you will not meet your Spending Plan the first few times you do it. (For me, it was the first few *years* I did it.) Remember you are learning a new skill, so be patient with yourself. When you overspend despite your efforts to follow your Spending Plan, think what might have happened if you hadn't even been *trying* or using a Spending Plan at all. Use the feedback the Actual Spending column gives you to make appropriate changes to next month's Spending Plan so it is attainable. When you look over your DIFFERENCE column, ask yourself how you'll handle these areas next month. Do you need to better manage some of your purchases? Or do you need to make a major life change such as taking in a room-mate or moving to a less expensive home? Can you increase your income? How soon can that happen? Take a moment to reflect on the information you've just gained and the changes you want to make.

WHERE DOES WORRY FIT?

If you normally worry about your money, now is the time to do it—for about five minutes. Then use the facts to come up with a plan and communicate that plan to the people who want to know (creditors, friends, loved ones, yourself). Once you finalize your Actual Spending Plan, all you need to do is follow it. No further worry required until next month! If you find yourself worrying throughout the month, use that energy to remind yourself how committed you are to following your Spending Plan and improving your situation.

WHAT ARE THE BENEFITS?

Continue using your Spending Plan even if you don't immediately see changes in your spending and saving behaviors. Why? First, the process gives you the accurate information you need to make the changes necessary to reach your financial goals. Second, it gives you repeated opportunities to look at your situation and decide what to do about it. When you're on track, you feel good about yourself and your money. When you're not, you have the information and tools to make an immediate change. Either way, it's essential to manage your money monthly!

GIVE ME ANOTHER REASON

There's another, less tangible benefit you'll notice. It has to do with this information sinking deep into your mind (your subconscious?) and effortlessly changing your behavior. If you have a genuine desire to meet your Spending Plan and you look at the information every month, your spending behavior subtly changes to accommodate your desire. It takes a little time for this to happen, but eventually it becomes second nature to follow your Spending Plan. Don't force it. Monthly repetition is the key.

In my case, I didn't try at all. It took a couple of years for it to sink in. A couple of years and a few raises, but now I am comfortable with my spending level relative to my income. My Cash to Burn easily lasts me through most weeks. I automatically know what extra expenses I can pay for this month and which ones I'll postpone to later months. It's effortless. You will achieve this faster than I did if you sincerely want it, are patient with yourself, and above all, if you manage your money monthly!

BACK TO BELLA

Bella has finished her first month's Spending Plan and is motivated to move on. Time can't pass fast enough for her to get out from under this credit card debt and have extra money left over for the fun things in life!

What are those, Bella?

Bella's preparing a complete list. Her first research spot is South of the Border—hot sun, tropical beaches, and cool dips on the dance floor. She's so ready her skin's tanning as she thinks about it!

Bella, it might be a little while before your debt is paid off and you've saved enough for the trip. Don't try to make these changes too fast or you might get discouraged and quit.

She'll consider that while she starts looking for a second job. With all these money skills she's learning maybe she'd have fun working part time in a bank, a CPA firm, or better yet— the IRS! Truthfully, she'd rather sing in the nightclub of a deluxe cruise ship bound for the tropics. A little more practice with her voice coach and *Love Boat* watch out!

SUMMARY

Using your Spending Plan each month gives repeated attention to your money and lets your desires gradually affect your spending behavior. You may use words to define other goals—with money you use numbers. The prosperity of your future results from your actions today. Make your Spending Plan part of your life now and watch the results.

TAKE ACTION

- Start working on your Spending Plan for next month. Play with it until it's realistic and your BOTTOM LINE is zero.

Part Two ❧

Develop Your Basic Money Management Skills

Your Spending Plan is the blueprint that guides your spending to reach your goals. But what about the basic money chores that are left? What practical steps help you streamline this work, combine it with creating your Spending Plans, and put your finances on cruise control for the rest of the month?

This section gives you a monthly process called Money Mechanics. You'll learn the four steps of Money Mechanics (including everything you ever wanted to know, and more, about balancing your checkbook), how to round, a simple filing system, and how to get all your paperwork together at once so you have everything you need when you sit down at your workspace.

But the real purpose of doing your Money Mechanics every month is to make time to think about your new money goals, the progress you've made, and how important these changes are to you. It's a process you can use for the rest of your life. Once you learn it, you may customize it to better suit your life (add electronic bill payments and software to do your calculations, discuss long-term goals with your partner, review your investment performance), but the steps of this routine will remain basically the same. So be sure to do your Money Mechanics monthly even if you don't see immediate results in your wallet. Learning the process and spending time with your money is what counts.

⸺ Chapter Eleven

Manage Your Money in Three Hours a Month

> *Money is a terrible master but an excellent servant.*
>
> —P. T. Barnum

Success with money requires: *knowledge*, which you are gaining now; *direction*, which takes the form of goals; and *action*, which you do monthly via your Money Mechanics, and daily as you make spending decisions. When you want to be beautiful you put time and attention into your looks. When you want to be healthy you put attention and energy into healthful activities. Money is the same—it likes attention. Money Mechanics is the *activity* of managing your money toward your goals. Like exercise, the goal is not to get strong and quit, but to get strong and stay strong. Just as continued exercise keeps your body strong, continued use of your Money Mechanics keeps your money strong.

MONEY MECHANICS—WHAT IS IT?

Money Mechanics involves four simple steps. Two of these steps (balancing your checkbook and paying your bills) are routine chores you need to do anyway. The other two steps turn your Spending Plan into a valuable feedback and planning device, as we've just covered. Here is the overview of the four steps in the Money Mechanics process, and how they all fit together:

1. *Balance Your Checkbook.*

   This necessary first step verifies that you have as much money in your checking account as you think you have. All is for naught if you start with the wrong number, so balance your checkbook first.

2. *Complete Last Month's Spending Plan.*

   Putting the actual dollars you spent next to the dollars you *planned* to spend reveals in which areas you followed your plan and in which areas you deviated. The Bottom Line, either positive or negative, rolls forward to next month's Spending Plan, giving you extra money to spend or a shortage to make up.

3. *Create Next Month's Spending Plan.*

   Here you list the expenses you plan to cover next month, make any adjustments, and calculate how much money goes toward your goals. Any feedback you gained from completing last month's Spending Plan is built into next month's Spending Plan.

4. *Pay Your Bills.*

   Routine, but necessary. After you create your Spending Plan you are free to write those checks and be done with everything until next month.

That's it. At one sitting you compare your actual spending to last month's plan, and set up a new plan for next month. All your bills are paid and your checkbook has the correct total of money in it. There is nothing left to do for the rest of the month but enjoy your spending!

MONEY MECHANICS—WHY IS IT IMPORTANT?

Positive Feedback Motivates

Completing last month's Spending Plan allows you time to pat yourself on the back for doing well. This is easy and automatic when your actual spending comes close to your planned spending. But even when it doesn't, give yourself credit because you're using the tool that helps you to do better next month. Success is on the way!

Easy Course Corrections

Course corrections get you back on track. Take time during your Money Mechanics to make any course corrections and adjustments in your spending patterns that become obvious after reviewing last month's Spending Plan. In areas where you deviated unfavorably from your planned spending, what can you do next month to stay on track? Are the assumptions in your Spending Plan valid? How well did they work? Is the Cash to Burn the right amount? Is your Flexible Money enough? Too much? This is the time to create new ideas and put them to work. Reviewing last month's Spending Plan gives you valuable feedback to make course corrections and keep yourself on track next month.

Adjust and Recommit to Goals

Working with your Spending Plan gives you the opportunity to recommit to your goals, a chance to keep them fresh in your mind, and to adjust them if necessary. Are your goals still important to you? Are they realistic, reasonable? Your Money Mechanics provides monthly motivation and a system to put your fresh enthusiasm into action.

Visualize Success

Visualize your Spending Plan coming in right on target, hold that picture in your mind, and manage your spending throughout the month so it happens. Money responds beautifully to constant and focused attention over a period of time. The repetition of working with your Spending Plan every month, combined with your own motivation, automatically changes your spending behavior because you're continually focusing on the same numbers. Imagine yourself completing your Spending Plan at the end of the month exactly as you planned, and watch it happen.

Money Likes to Be Organized

This is no secret. Wealthy people and corporations know this. The profession of accounting was created to organize money for both these groups. Rest easy, you don't need to be an accountant (or think like one) to master some simplified tricks of the trade for organizing your personal funds. Learning to organize and watch your money at the basic level gives you the confidence required to learn what you need for higher levels of financial management. Once you learn the basics, you can expand into more advanced areas if you like because the same tools apply. Wealthy people *must* acquire more knowledge about money than the rest of us, whether they like it or not. *It is a necessity for them.* If you're planning on gaining riches, you *will need to gain knowledge.* Here's your starting point!

Be with Your Money

You enjoy spending time with the people and things you like (a lover, a new car, friends, good food). This is the time to be with your money. Relax and enjoy this time together. Get comfortable and used to the process so you look forward to spending the few hours it takes each month. When you are happy to be with your money, your money will be happy to be with you, and you will find it stays around longer than it used to.

See Everything at Once

Your Money Mechanics session let's you see everything that affects your money situation at once. Your money becomes familiar to you as you decide how to manage it. You cover all the bases, since you do both your financial housework (balancing your checkbook and paying your bills) and your planning together. Each affects the other so you'll have no surprises later on. On one sheet, all your inflows and outflows are listed. With last month's progress fresh in your mind, you can make changes for next month, put it together, and see for yourself how it will be accomplished.

Easy Fun

You'll soon become an expert at doing your Money Mechanics and it will be easy and fun for you. Any uncertainties you once had about your money will be replaced with confidence. You won't understand how you ever managed without your Money Mechanics. You'll look forward to the once-a-month ritual and wish it wasn't over so quickly.

GET SET FOR SUCCESS

Are these enough reasons why Money Mechanics is good for you? Crucial to your financial success? Even fun and enjoyable? Now a few words about the logistics.

Make sure you have two to three hours of uninterrupted time to do your Money Mechanics. This is necessary to keep the continuity of the numbers well focused in your mind as you move from one step to the next. Self-designated breaks are fine, but unwelcome interruptions cause errors that can easily discourage and frustrate you. I enjoy spending a quiet weekday evening or a Saturday morning doing my Money Mechanics.

You will need a clear desk or workspace. Allow yourself enough room. If you don't have a desk, use your kitchen table. Clear it off. Be sure you are comfortable. Put some relaxing music on in the background and start with a cup of your favorite tea or coffee. Gather together everything you'll need so you won't interrupt yourself at the wrong time for supplies. This includes your checkbook, your shoebox (details later), and your binder containing your Spending Plans. You'll also need a calendar, a calculator, plenty of colored pens, a pencil and an eraser, stamps, a wastebasket, and envelopes.

Bella can't wait to start. *WHOOSH!* Her kitchen table becomes financial headquarters and she's ready for *action!*

SUMMARY

Money Mechanics is the activity of managing your money toward your goals. Master your Money Mechanics and make it a lifetime habit that will take you wherever you want to go with your money. Using Money Mechanics lets you make all your money decisions at one time each month and puts you on autopilot to carry them out. It frees you to focus on growing your money or concentrating on other values in your life. Whether you want more prosperity or just more simplification and freedom from money worries and chores, doing your Money Mechanics monthly is the solution!

TAKE ACTION

- Buy a calculator if you don't already own one. It's a good investment!

Chapter Twelve

Balancing a Checkbook in Ten Minutes

Trust in Allah, but tie your camel.

—Moslem saying

I've bounced only two checks. One was to a grocery store, the other was to pay for my CPA license. That's right—my CPA license. You can understand why I now balance my checkbook as soon as I get the bank statement. No more problems, no more bounced checks, a current CPA license, and it takes just ten minutes a month.

THE GOOD NEWS IS . . .

It's going to be a lot easier to balance, or double-check, your bank statement now than ever before. Why? You are writing fewer checks, and you are writing them early in the month. By the time you receive your bank statement, there are almost *no* checks outstanding to cause a difference. The purpose of balancing your bank statement is to find differences between the total you show in your checkbook and the total the bank shows on its statement. You want to know about any errors made either by you or the bank *before* you plan next month's spending.

Those of you who already balance your checkbook at the speed of light every month can skip directly to *Helpful Hints for Better Balancing* at the end of this chapter, then move on. The rest of us will go through the balancing act, step by step. By the end of this section, *everyone* will balance their checkbooks in a flash.

WHY BOTHER?

In over ten years of balancing my checkbook I have never found a bank error, but I have discovered—hard to believe—a few of my own. Only by checking my numbers to the bank's numbers could I find and correct my error. This is the value of balancing your checkbook every month. If you make an error, you know about it *before* moving forward to your Spending Plans. If the bank makes a mistake, you notify them.

Sometime during the month your bank may make a deduction from your account for a service or check printing fee, or add money for interest. You need to adjust your own records by these amounts, or you won't have the correct total in your checkbook. The balancing process ensures you stay current with these adjustments each month.

AN OVERVIEW

The main reason you and your bank have different totals for the money in your account is because the bank's information always lags behind the *updated* balance in your checkbook. As long as you make transactions to your account *after* the bank sends you your statement, there will always be a difference. A check takes a few days to float through our banking system, so checks you wrote that have not reached your bank are not included on your monthly statement.

Any amounts in your checkbook that are not on the bank's statement are called *outstanding items*. It is necessary to list them separately to balance your checkbook total to the bank statement total. Since the *Money Without Madness System* of managing money creates *fewer* outstanding checks, the time it takes to balance your checkbook is reduced.

Balance your checkbook soon after your bank statement arrives and you will have fewer outstanding items to create differences. The longer you wait, the more checks you write and the more complicated it becomes. Balance your checkbook the week you get your statement and make life easier!

THE EASY PROCESS

Here are the steps to balance your checkbook:

1. Use a calculator to calculate the total in your checkbook through the last transaction. Do this twice to make sure you've got the right total. (If you like to keep an updated total throughout the month, *always* use a calculator, and *always* do it twice.)

2. On your bank statement, circle the ending balance or total on the last day the statement covers. You'll need this later.

3. Go through your bank statement's listing of checks that have cleared. Using a pen, make a check mark in your register next to the amount of each cleared check. There is a small preprinted column next to the amount column just for this purpose. It shows a check mark at the top. (Use different colored pens each month in case you have to go back over your work. This makes it easy to determine which checks cleared during which month.) Most bank statements list the checks in numerical order so it is quick and easy to run through their listing in the same order as your checkbook. Don't concern yourself with the check *numbers* —look only at the *amounts*. Make sure the *amount* the bank shows agrees with the amount in your checkbook. If it doesn't, circle it and keep going.

Don't stop until you've completed this step. Work continually *from* your statement *to* your check register—never in the reverse.

4. Go to the next section on your bank statement and do the same thing. It may be called Deposits, Other Debits, or Other Credits. (In bank lingo, *debits* take money away from your account and *credits* add to it.) Do not skip a section or you will miss something critical. Do not let anyone interrupt you or you may lose your place and forget which sections you covered.

5. If you come across any item listed on the bank statement but not in your checkbook, circle it and keep going. When you finish going through the statement, go back and figure out why these items are listed on your bank statement and not in your checkbook. If it is a service charge, check charge, interest paid to you, or an automatic deduction (insurance payments), list it in your checkbook and add or subtract it from your total as appropriate. If it is a check you wrote but didn't enter in your checkbook, include it now and update your total—likewise with any ATM withdrawals you made but forgot to list in your checkbook.

Time for a break? Sure—take a break. When you return it's time for an explanation. Remember those outstanding items we mentioned earlier—checks, deposits, and ATM withdrawals that are in your checkbook but *not* on the bank statement? By putting check marks next to the items that are listed on your statement, you have made it easy to recognize the outstanding items—the ones *without* the check marks.

6. Turn one of your statement pages over to the worksheet preprinted on the back. Here comes the Moment of Truth—are you ready? Using this worksheet, do the following:

a. Work from your checkbook now and list all outstanding checks, ATM transactions, and anything else you see that *lowers* your bank balance in the section provided for outstanding checks. Round the pennies up or down. (If you're uncomfortable about rounding—hold that thought. We'll cover rounding further in Chapter 16 on Creative Rounding.) Add the items and put the total at the bottom of the section. Add them with your calculator and do it twice if you want to finish quickly and without problems.

b. List any outstanding deposits in the other box provided. Usually this is a smaller box. Total these. All the items in your checkbook without check marks should be listed in one of these two boxes.

c. Follow the worksheet and list the bank statement's ending balance. This is the amount you circled on the first page. It is the last total listed, not the total listed at the beginning of the month.

d. List the total of your outstanding deposits and *add* it to the bank statement balance. *Use a calculator and do it twice.*

e. List the total of your outstanding checks and *subtract* it from the number you just calculated. Enter this amount on the last line, usually called Your Current Checkbook Balance.

f. Guess what? The last number should be the same as the last total listed in your checkbook. It is? Great! Congratulate yourself. Write something in your checkbook next to the total to indicate you balanced to the bank statement. Simply writing "Balanced" is fine, but I usually put some stars and exclamation points (* ! * ! *) along with it.

BUT WAIT

The numbers are *not the same?* This happens occasionally to everyone. After practice it will be rare. But right now, let's fix it.

Most of the time the difference will be caused by an error made by *you* rather than the bank, simply because the bank is using a computer and you are not. However, there are a number of tricks to help you find errors quickly. Here are the steps to take when your checkbook and your bank statement don't agree.

A. Check your math. Check the addition and subtraction on the balancing worksheet on the back of your statement. Then check your checkbook balance *since you last balanced* by adding all deposits and subtracting all checks that follow. (This is why it's handy to make a notation when you balance.) If all math is correct, try the next step.

B. Find the difference between the two numbers that are supposed to be equal. Which one is higher? Is the difference significant? In other words, do you recognize the amount? Often an overlooked item causes you to be off. Think about the difference and look for an item that is the same amount. If you find it, think about how to correct it. Step C. will help.

C. Which total is greater? If you are showing a higher number in your checkbook than the bank is showing, what could be the cause? Perhaps the bank deducted a service fee you forgot to subtract from your checkbook. Look for the amount of the service fee. Did you enter it and subtract it from your checkbook? Perhaps you have a deposit the bank doesn't yet show. If you do, it should be listed as an Outstanding Item. Is it? Or . . .

D. Is your checkbook total lower than the bank's total? What could be the cause? Is there a check that hasn't cleared the bank yet, that you forgot to include in your listing of outstanding checks? Look through your checkbook for a check equal to the amount you are off. Sometimes these are on a different page than the rest of the outstanding checks, so you may have to go back several pages in your checkbook. Has the bank given you a credit for some interest earned that you didn't add to your checkbook total? If none of these steps leads to success, read on.

E. You need to recheck your work from beginning to end. (Yes, that's right—from beginning to end.) Before starting this, take a break. Get up and walk around. Breathe deeply. Let the cat out. Clear your mind so you will start fresh when you return. With a clear mind, sit down and think again about the amount causing the difference and what it could be. If the answer doesn't come to you, then begin to recheck your work from Step 1 under *The Easy Process.* Cross-check the check marks in your check register as you go through a second time instead of relying on your first check mark. That could be the source of the error. (A cross-check draws a slash (\) through the original check mark.) Follow each step carefully, going slower than you did at first, and you should come out right.

YOUR FIRST TIME

Getting started can be overwhelming, especially if you've had your bank account for a long time and never balanced it. Do you have to go all the way back to the beginning to get it right? No. What's done is history and not critical in working toward your first balancing.

Using the last *three* months of bank statements, put a check mark in your checkbook next to each item that has cleared the bank. Add and subtract bank charges not previously entered. Now turn over your latest statement and follow the worksheet balancing instructions. List as outstanding anything that is not checked off in your checkbook but was entered *within the last three months only.* Calculate the total and compare it to your checkbook total. How close do you come?

Quickly follow the guidelines for finding a difference but do *not* do the whole thing over again. If you are *reasonably* close, change your checkbook balance. Make your checkbook total equal to the total on your *balancing worksheet—not* the total on the front of the bank statement—and move on.

You may find it takes a couple of months before you are easily balancing your bank statement to your checkbook on the first try. Not to worry—this is normal. Stay with it. After doing it for about three months, you'll be on track!

HELPFUL HINTS FOR BETTER CHECKBOOK BALANCING

Here's a summary of the main points to remember when balancing your checkbook:

1. *Always* use a calculator to determine the total in your checkbook. Calculate the numbers *twice* to make sure you've done it correctly. This will eliminate ninety percent of the differences between your checkbook and the bank's total and will take you much less time than finding a math error at the end of the month. Do not total each new entry in your checkbook, but put the updated total at the end of each page and at the end of your entries on the day you balance to the bank statement. Since you now manage your money according to your Spending Plan, not your checkbook, there is no need to have an updated total throughout the month. It is necessary only for balancing.

2. Balance your checkbook as the *first* step of your Money Mechanics each month. That way you don't have a lot of uncleared checks to list as outstanding items. If you pay all your bills first, you have a new figure to balance to. All those checks become outstanding items, creating many more places for errors to occur.

3. Round to the nearest dollar when listing outstanding checks and deposits. We'll talk about rounding in Chapter 16 because it saves you time in several areas of managing your money.

4. Save time by omitting the check numbers and payees when listing your outstanding checks on the balancing worksheet. Most checks will clear next month, so you won't need this information. The amount is all you need to retrace to the original check. An exception is your ATM withdrawals, which are likely to be the same amounts. Put the transaction date next to each amount so you know which ones are outstanding. If you have several deposits of the same amount (paychecks, for instance) use the date to identify those as well.

5. Make a special mark in your checkbook next to the balanced figure. This is helpful if you need to go back to a point when you and the bank were in agreement. I write * ! *Balanced* ! * on the line of the correct balance.

6. Use the forms on the back of your bank statement. They are well-designed and convenient. Your balancing work stays with the statement and takes no extra room in your filing system.

7. If your bank stores copies of your checks on microfiche instead of returning them to you, use checks that create automatic duplicates. This makes it easier to find the amount of any checks you may have overlooked and list them in your checkbook.

8. When marking checks that have cleared the bank, always use the *amount* of the check instead of the check number. This way you automatically make sure the bank recorded the amount correctly and did not add a zero or transpose numbers. Checks are entered into the system by human hands so an error is possible, especially if your writing is hard to read.

9. Always work *from* your bank statement *to* your checkbook when marking off items, and move in sequential order. This assures you that *everything* listed on the statement has a match in your checkbook. If it doesn't, circle it and keep going. After you have gone through the whole statement, work on discrepancies.

Bella thinks this is some chapter. All those 1-2-3's and ABC's. She's glad she's already successful with her checkbook balancing and could skip past most of it. The Helpful Hints were interesting though, and will save her time. Especially Number Four and Number Five.

SUMMARY

With the *Money Without Madness System*, balancing your checkbook is faster and easier than ever before. You'll look forward to receiving your bank statements each month and starting your Money Mechanics. It takes only five to ten minutes to complete your checkbook balancing once you get the hang of it!

TAKE ACTION

- Open your checkbook and locate the small column with a check mark at the top.

- Turn over one of your bank statements. Find and study the worksheet there.

Chapter Thirteen

A Fast and Easy Way to Pay Your Bills

*Anyone who says he doesn't want more money
will lie about other things too.*

—A wise man or a cynic?

Does the mail too often bring those unpleasant requests for *your* hard earned bucks? Instead of realizing you'd rather buy a car phone, ten new CDs, or just take a quiet trip to your favorite beachside B&B (away from bill collectors), these companies expect you to pay for something you bought *last* month. (What *did* you buy anyway? It's hard to remember!) Do your bills come at different and inconvenient times during the month and get lost *very* easily? If you accidentally forget to send your payment do you get endless reminders in the mail—some even threatening to *cut you off* if you don't pay?

IS THIS ANY WAY TO LIVE YOUR LIFE?

Of course not. Let's bring some order to this scene, so you can get some control of bill payments—fast! From now on, you'll toss those bills into your fancy financial filing system without even *opening* them, without a second thought. Once a month when you do the easiest part of your Money Mechanics, you'll take care of them *all at once* and be done with it! So get ready for the last step of your Money Mechanics: *Pay Your Bills.*

FASTER THAN A SPEEDING TICKET!

Gather all bills and slips of paper. To save time, go through each step completely with every bill, then move on to the next step.

There's nothing difficult or complicated about paying your bills, since you've already created your Spending Plan and *know exactly what you're going to pay.* Your goal with this last step is simply to get the paperwork finished quickly and correctly. When it comes to paying bills, our motto is: Do It Fast, Do It Right, Do It Once! Here are some timesaving tips to speed the process and some paperwork tips to make sure the same bill doesn't come back to haunt you next month.

1. Open the bills you haven't yet opened. Throw out any extra paper, keeping only the bill, the remittance slip, and the return envelope.

2. Look over the amounts and make sure they are right. Make sure your payments from last month have been credited to your account correctly. Review your phone bill and wonder why it's so high.

3. Circle the correct amount to pay and write it in the box on the remittance slip. Be careful to only circle the *Current* Amount Due instead of the *Total* Amount Due if you paid last month's bill and the payment hasn't been credited yet on your new bill. Otherwise you'll pay last month's bill twice without realizing it and spend extra time trying to figure it out later.

4. Write out your checks and place each one with the right bill. Record each check in your checkbook as you write it.

Let me interrupt to add a word about interruptions. Distracting aren't they? They're also disruptive to this part of your Money Mechanics. If life wants to interrupt you when you're paying your bills, just say "Give me a second" without stopping your work. Finish the step you're on and when you're ready, give all your attention to the interruption. Now, give all your attention back to . . .

5. Go through the pile once more, putting the checks and remittance slips in the envelopes (make sure the address shows through). Seal the envelopes.

6. Pass through the pile once more, stamping your return address on the envelopes. Put a postage stamp on each one, and you're done. Simple. Pop them in the mail.

And speaking of mailing, if your income arrives steadily throughout the month and you need to spread your payments out similarly, you can still complete the work of writing your checks all at once. Just add this step:

7. Write the date to *mail* each payment on the back of its envelope. Put a reminder on your calendar or day timer, or a Post-it™ note on your bathroom mirror, car mirror, fridge door, or front door reminding you to mail each payment on the correct day.

AND DON'T YOU COME BACK NO MORE, NO MORE

What else do you need to know to make sure this is a Do-It-Fast, Do-It-Right, Do-It-Once event?

1. Companies usually include a remittance slip with their bills. Use these slips. This makes sure your payment goes where it's supposed to. More importantly, it gives the company your name, account number, and the bill

you are paying so they are sure to give you credit for your payment.

2. The slips have a box labeled *Amount Included*. Some people write *Yes*. The correct answer is to write the amount you are sending them. Do this. It helps the company control their receipts and it ensures you get credit for the full amount of your check.

3. Write your account number in the memo area on the face of your check. This is a key step many people overlook. If your check gets separated from the remittance slip, you will still get proper credit. This is especially helpful if your last name is a common one or a relative also has an account with the same company. (*Hint*: When you send a check to the IRS, always put your social security number in the memo area for the same reason.)

Following the above steps helps the company process your check directly, correctly, and quickly to your account. You reduce the chance of spending time later figuring out which payment they missed, and sending copies of canceled checks to keep your account straight.

One more thing—get an address stamp or labels. They are cheap and save you time. If you pay more than five bills a month, make this purchase.

THREE-, SIX-, AND TWELVE-MONTH BILLS

Estimated tax payments, health insurance premiums, property taxes, and auto insurance may be billed quarterly or annually instead of monthly. What's the best way to handle these payments? The safest way is to set up a separate account to save the money for these payments. Each month transfer the correct *monthly* amount into that account. When you get the bill, make your payment from this account. Simple. If you'd rather not set up a separate account, apply the same concept to your savings account. Add the monthly amount of any periodic bills to your monthly savings deposit and use a check from this account to pay the bill when it is due.

If you don't trust yourself to set aside the right amount of money each month, try arranging to have the company bill you monthly. Some mortgage companies collect an estimate for property taxes along with the monthly mortgage payment. While you may not like the idea of someone else getting the interest on this money, it can be worth it when the alternative is to come up with a large tax payment on short notice. If your health insurance company will bill monthly or quarterly, choose monthly. Will your auto insurance company allow monthly payments if you pay a finance charge? The small added cost may be worth the convenience to you.

Bella thinks this sounds a lot easier than paying her bills on a catch-as-catch-can basis, especially since her bills never stay in one place, but tend to get easily lost in piles of mail, under sofa cushions, and especially inside magazines and books. Paying them all at once sounds great, but how to *find* them all at once is what she wants to know.

Bella, keep reading. The next chapter tells all!

SUMMARY

That's it! So easy, it's even fun. What a nice feeling to know your bills aren't going to get one more second of your attention until the same time next month!

TAKE ACTION:

- Order an address stamp or labels.

- Buy enough postage stamps to last for three months of mailing bills.

- Buy a box of plain white envelopes for payments that need them.

Chapter Fourteen

A Filing System that Works for You

I love being a writer. What I can't stand is the paperwork.

—Peter De Vries

It's true! You don't need anything fancier than the classic shoebox to keep a necessary amount of order to do your Money Mechanics *and* eliminate money-related stress. Anything financial that comes in during the month goes right in the shoebox. This includes bills, bank statements, mail-order forms, charge slips, deposit receipts, medical claim forms, and coupon books for loan payments. Bills don't even get opened. You don't care how much they are! At the end of the month you have *all* the relevant information you need in one place instead of looking for bits and pieces of paper that are lost somewhere. You know where everything is when you need it—in your shoebox!

NO CLUTTER!

Keep your shoebox free from everything but financial paper-work and some items you need for your Money Mechanics (your calculator, postage stamps, and your address stamp). You want everything in order and at your fingertips so you can buzz right through the work. (Your Spending Plans won't fit neatly into the shoebox, so keep them in a three-ring binder.) If you have a fixed payment to make to someone who doesn't bill you (rent, church pledges, loan payments to Ma and Pa), put a piece of paper in your shoebox with the payment amount and the address to remind you to make that payment with the rest of your bills.

Remember, *do not* put your entire pile of mail in the shoebox or you will clutter it up and create added work for yourself uncluttering it at the end of the month. Keep your shoebox out of sight so you are not tempted to think about anything other than how well your Spending Plan is going during the month. I keep my financial shoebox in my top right desk drawer next to the shoebox that holds my pens and pencils (I like shoeboxes).

CLEAN IT OUT

After you pay your bills at the end of the month, take any remaining paperwork out of your shoebox. Toss out what you don't need anymore and file any items you want to keep *in a separate file*. An exception is the slips of paper reminding you to pay those folks who don't bill you. These stay in the shoebox until you no longer make that payment. It's critical to clear the shoebox once a month so you don't mix your paid bills with the incoming ones. Leaving unnecessary paperwork in your shoebox not only is messy and confusing, but might cause you to mistakenly pay something twice if you are not careful.

This raises the question: What do you keep, and for how long? Here are some guidelines.

KEEPERS

Keep your bank statements. If you are ever audited by one of our friendly IRS agents these may help. After five years you can toss them out unless you have intentionally defrauded the IRS. Then your returns are still open for scrutiny. You decide.

Keep your credit card statements for a similar time period if you have deducted anything for taxes. They can be used as documentation. Even if you don't deduct any credit card purchases on your tax returns, it is a good idea to keep the statements for at least six months to a year in case you have a dispute with the company and need to go back over your records.

Keep statements that still have an open balance: an annual insurance premium paid monthly, medical statements that are copaid by a health insurance carrier, and car loans. Keep these until you receive a statement showing credit for your last payment. Once that shows up, you may toss out the statement if the only activity on it is your payments. Keep medical statements if you expect insurance payments to be made later so you have complete documentation in case the insurance company doesn't (hard to believe, but it happens). Keep any statement with a disputed item on it until the dispute is settled.

Hint: If you are making payments toward a balance, get into the habit of writing the check number, amount, and date you sent the check on the portion of the statement *you keep.* This saves you the time and trouble of looking it up if the company doesn't give you credit for your check. You simply tell them, "I paid $102.86 with check number 1234 on June 2. It should have been posted to my account soon thereafter." Who can argue? This is especially helpful with your credit card statements.

Keep deposit receipts from the ATM machine until you get your bank statement and see the deposit amount correctly entered by the bank. Then kiss 'em good-bye. You may want to keep your withdrawal slips if you have withdrawn varying amounts of money. Then toss them out as soon as you've balanced your bank statement to your checkbook and everything matches.

Keep receipts from your credit card purchases. Yes, store these little treasures in your shoebox until the statement shows up. If the amounts are correct and you aren't deducting these items on your tax returns—adios!

WHAT TO TOSS OUT

Any bill you pay in full can be tossed out, provided you don't need it for tax deductions. This includes utility bills, phone bills, health club bills, etc. You don't need to save these for any financial reason, so why keep the extra paper?

Bella loves the idea of not opening her bills until the end of the month. This is exactly what she always wanted to do anyway. She's searching for just the right shoebox to fill this important place in her new life of financial ease. She thinks she may need to buy those soft, gray suede flats to get just the right designer box.

SUMMARY

The best way to deal with your financial paperwork is all at once, when you're ready for it. Not a moment sooner. All it takes is a good shoebox, a hiding place, some well-planned procrastination, and you're set. Oh, one more thing—you need to coordinate the timing of your bills so they all come due *after* you do your Money Mechanics. How? The next chapter explains.

TAKE ACTION

- Find a shoebox.

- Put all your financial items and paperwork into it.

- Make a place for it in a drawer where you won't see it until you want to.

Chapter Fifteen

Fit Your Bills into Your Calendar

God grant me the serenity to accept the things I cannot change.

—from R. Niebuhr's Serenity Prayer

. . . And the money to pay my bills at one time.

—Karen Brigham

When is the best time each month to do your Money Mechanics? Does it seem like your bills arrive and are due on various days throughout the month? Even if they were coordinated, could your checking account bear those heavy payments all at once, or would the balance crumble, never to rise again?

To do your Money Mechanics you need your bills and your bank statement together at one time. But they don't have to *come* to you at once. With your new shoebox in place and some scheduling changes, you will find the right time of the month to do your Money Mechanics. One that allows you to pay most of your bills at once and on time.

CONSTANT OR VARYING?

What checks do you write and when are they due? Do the amounts vary or stay constant? Do you receive a bill or use a book of coupons as with mortgage payments? Bills that are for the same amount every month such as mortgage and car payments, rent, club dues, and loans do not affect the timing of your Money Mechanics. Since you know the amount, you put it into your Spending Plan and write the check without waiting for the bill. Just keep the check in your shoebox until the bill arrives, then send it off.

You need bills for monthly payments that vary in amount. Credit card, phone, and utility bills are examples of these. Three tactics help you coordinate these bills so you have the information you need when you want it. If the bill comes *before* you are ready to do your Money Mechanics, put it in your shoebox until you need it. If the bill comes later than you want it to, request a change in the billing date. If your request isn't accommodated, estimate the amount for your Spending Plan and wait until next month to pay the actual bill.

CREDIT CARD BILLS—IT'S ABOUT TIME

Major bank credit cards are flexible with their billing cycles. All you need to do is make the request. Pick a day you'd like to receive your credit card bill, allowing plenty of time to return the payment by the new due date. Call the 800 number on your bill and ask to change your billing cycle. The representative may change it over the phone or ask you to send a request in writing. Either way, it's simple and it's done. This is good news since you must have the bill to know the amount to pay and you don't want to be late with these payments.

WHEREFORE ART THOU, BANK STATEMENT?

Balancing your checkbook is the first step of your Money Mechanics, so you need to receive your bank statement on time. When does yours arrive? Banks generally run personal statements on the last day of the month. Make note of the day your statement arrives. How close is it to the end of the month? If the timing delays your Money Mechanics, call your bank and ask them to run it before the end of the month, on the twenty-fifth or twenty-seventh. This gets it to you sooner and your balancing works just as well. It doesn't matter what date you balance to, as long as you do it once a month.

CALL THEM ON IT

Are there other bills you'd like to receive earlier or later? Call the company's billing department and ask the following questions:

- *When is the payment due? (Yes, there is a date on the bill, but sometimes there is a grace period given but not shown.)*

- *When will a late charge be added to my account? How much is it?*

- *When is information on late payments reported to credit bureaus?*

- *Is there any flexibility in the billing cycle so I can receive the bill sooner (or later) to accommodate my schedule and pay it on time?*

It's important to know when, if ever, these companies report you to credit bureaus for late payments. I don't recommend jeopardizing a good credit history for the sake of convenience since you can have both. You may be surprised at the answers you get. I discovered that my phone and utility companies don't report to credit bureaus unless the account is closed without final payment. One December I paid only half of a $140 phone bill and received no late notices at all from the phone company. However, a finance charge of a few dollars showed up on January's bill. I was glad to pay this small amount for the convenience of stretching my payment during Christmas.

HOT AND COLD SWINGS

Some utility companies offer billing programs that spread payments out evenly over a three-, six-, or twelve-month period, smoothing the costs of changing weather. Request this billing program if it works better for you.

ESTIMATE LATE BILLS

If a bill arrives late and you're unsuccessful in changing the timing, use an estimate for your Spending Plan. Be sure to estimate high enough so you build in good news instead of bad news when you get the bill. When the bill arrives, you can either pay it right away or put it into your shoebox to pay during your next Money Mechanics session. I prefer filing it unopened to keep my mind free of bills until the end of the month.

PLAY AROUND

My guess is that most of your bills arrive near the end of the month, and that will be the best time to do your Money Mechanics. Play around with the timing of your Money Mechanics for a couple of months until you find what works. While you do this, make sure to pay on time the bills that charge you interest. Where possible, rearrange payment dates to fit your schedule. I do my Money Mechanics any time during the first week of the month and still pay my bills within thirty days of their date. The only bills I changed were my two credit cards. Another company always sends their bill too late and gets paid the following month. Since this is within thirty days from the date they send the bill it creates no problem for them.

AUTOMATIC REMINDER SYSTEM

Notice the last bill you receive every month and use it to remind yourself you have all the paperwork you need to start your Money Mechanics. My bank statement always arrives after the rest of my bills. As soon as I get it, I plan to do my Money Mechanics. That way I am reminded automatically by my mail and put no thought into it until I have everything I need.

THE COMFORT OF A CASH CUSHION

Where will the money come from when you convert to paying all your bills at once? Most people with tight cash flows are used to timing the release of their payments to the receipt of their paychecks. This works fine if you're used to it, but requires attention throughout the month. Instead, imagine sending off all your payments at once, knowing they're taken care of and you can forget about bills until the same time next month. This is the luxury of having enough money in your account to cover your payments no matter when your paycheck arrives. This is the luxury of having a Cash Cushion to sink into.

Does a Cash Cushion cost you? Not at all. This money doesn't *go anywhere*. It stays right in your checking account as *part of your savings*. At the beginning of the month you dip into it, and throughout the month, as your paychecks get deposited and not spent on bills, it is replenished. It never leaves, it is just used and replenished.

HOW MUCH DO YOU NEED?

A guideline for the amount of your Cash Cushion is your Total Expenses less one paycheck. We'll use Bella's situation to illustrate:

Pay Frequency	Weekly	Biweekly	Semimonthly	Monthly
Total Expenses	$1,500	$1,500	$1,500	$1,500
Less One Paycheck	-346	-692	-750	-1,500
Cash Cushion Needed	$1,154	$808	$750	0

Notice you don't need a Cash Cushion when you are paid once a month since all your cash is received at the beginning of the month.

HOW MUCH DO YOU HAVE?

You may have some money right now to build your Cash Cushion. Where? Any money in your checking account *before* you start your first month of the *Money Without Madness System* is your beginning Cash Cushion, as long as it is not earmarked to use next month. How do you figure out how much it is? By following these steps:

Right before you start your first month of using your Spending Plan, do your bank balancing and come to a correct total in your checkbook. When Bella does this, on the fourth day of the month, she comes to a total of $1,082. Next, back out any transactions that will be needed for next month's Spending Plan. You may have to back out a paycheck or portion of one (see Chapter 10, *Putting Your Spending Plan to Work* for an explanation on backing out transactions). Bella's semimonthly paycheck of $750 was deposited to her account on the first of the month. Since she'll use this as income for next month, she backs out this amount leaving a new total of $332. This is the starting amount of Bella's Cash Cushion.

BUILDING YOUR CASH CUSHION

How do you add to your Cash Cushion after you've started using your Spending Plan every month? Bella's off to a good start with her $332 of Cash Cushion, but it's not enough to let her mail all her bill payments at the beginning of the month then forget about them. Because she is paid semimonthly, she needs $750 as her Cash Cushion. To build your Cash Cushion, simply list on your Spending Plan the amount you wish to add each month on the line START SAVING NOW! but don't transfer it to a savings account. This way it stays in your checking account to build your Cash Cushion.

NEGATIVE CUSHIONS

What if you come up with a negative number when you calculate your Cash Cushion? If Bella had finished her bank balancing with a total of $632 and subtracted the paycheck belonging to the next month of $750, she'd have a negative Cash Cushion of $118. Now what?

Follow the same instructions for building a Cash Cushion. However, until you've eliminated the negative Cash Cushion, use extra care in timing the release of your payments since you're operating in the red. Make it your first priority to contribute enough each month under START SAVING NOW! to remove the negative sign and fluff up your Cash Cushion to a comfortable amount.

IT'S INVISIBLE

Since you'll never spend your Cash Cushion, there's no need to include it on your Spending Plan. It provides temporary help with cash flow only, it's not money to spend. Keep it invisible to your Spending Plan.

Bella is in favor of keeping a Cash Cushion in her account. She looks forward to spending when she's inspired to instead of practicing patience until the next paycheck arrives. And she likes the convenience of thinking about bills only once a month.

SUMMARY

Coordinating your bills so all the information is available at one time helps you better plan your spending. Building a Cash Cushion into your account so you can pay everything at once is a benefit well worth investing in. When your Cash Cushion is small, you need to spread your expenses evenly through the month. When you have a full Cash Cushion, you can spend anytime you want. Make building a Cash Cushion your first savings goal so that when it comes to timing and convenience, you *have it your way!*

TAKE ACTION

- Record the receipt and due dates of your bills as they come in this month.

- Identify the best time to do your Money Mechanics each month.

- Request changes in billing dates if necessary.

- Calculate the Cash Cushion you'll need.

- At the end of this month, determine how much Cash Cushion you already have.

Part Three

Making the Most of Your Money

If you earn a steady paycheck, have no problems with your taxes, and share your money comfortably with your favorite charities and your favorite spouse, this section is optional. If not, you'll find some helpful hints in the next few chapters.

For entrepreneurs and salespeople who don't always know how much their month-to-month incomes will be, these chapters offer solutions. If you do everything else right, but you forget Uncle Sam, your money goals are shot. Read the brief chapter on taxes. For anyone who's ever considered taking the tithing plunge, yours truly offers a testimonial. And lastly, for those of you who want to mix your money with the love of your life (for extra fireworks), you can choose from three ways to do it while still keeping a Spending Plan and doing your Money Mechanics. But first, let's explore the pros and pitfalls of chasing down digits south of the decimal.

Chapter Sixteen

Creative Rounding Saves You Time

A little knowledge is a dangerous thing.
—Proverb

A little money is worse.
—Karen Brigham

Rounding makes your financial work easier and faster to complete. It simplifies the numbers you are working with, gives you fewer digits to record, and makes significant numbers easier to remember. Some numbers you will round to the nearest dollar and others to the nearest five or ten dollars. There are other numbers you won't round at all.

ROUND ABOUT NOW

Round to the nearest *dollar* when listing outstanding checks on your bank balancing worksheet and the actual numbers in your Spending Plan at the end of the month. Both of these documents are for your eyes only, so you don't need precision to the penny. Listing each check amount exactly as it is written, including the pennies, takes more time to write, more time to add, and you gain nothing from the extra level of accuracy. Your checkbook balancing is easier and faster to complete once you start rounding.

Here's a quick review of rounding to the nearest dollar: Anything from 1 to 49 pennies is rounded down or dropped, anything from 50 to 99 pennies is rounded up. Some examples are:

Actual Number		*Rounded Number*
$ 1.14	(my pocket change)	$ 1
$ 385.53	(one cross-country airline trip)	$ 386
$ 575.25	(one cross-town trip to my auto mechanic)	$ 575
$ 1,467.49	(Bill Gates's pocket change)	$ 1,467
$ 31,538.91	(your monthly income?)	$ 31,539

By following this technique, you are *guaranteed* to come within one or two dollars of the same answer you would if you used the actual amount. The point is, within one or two dollars is acceptable here. Don't get fanatical about accuracy to the penny with your Money Mechanics.

And speaking of accuracy, when you finish balancing your checkbook and find you match your bank statement within one or two dollars, or anything up to five dollars, should you go back and find the difference? No! Let it go. Move on. A difference this small will not bankrupt you or even throw you off next month. Your time is worth more than the five dollars you are looking for. Not to mention the added frustration created when you think you are off in your work when instead, you are done!

ROUND PEG, SQUARE HOLE

When dealing with the outside world the rounding rule doesn't apply. Why? Because most computerized accounting systems are programmed to take pennies just as seriously as thousands of dollars. If you receive a bill for $17.12 and take the liberty of rounding down to $17, you create an outstanding balance of $.12. The computer automatically sends you a bill for $.12 month after month even though the postage costs more than the bill. Sounds crazy, but with so many customers, these companies might lose money if people weren't consistent. Close enough is not good enough when paying your bills. Be precise.

I also recommend you record the checks in your checkbook complete with pennies, for two reasons. One, it is easier to quickly eyeball the cleared checks from your bank statement at the end of the month. Two, it's a good idea to have an accurate record of your check amounts in case you need to contact a company or ask the bank to supply you with a microfiche copy.

GIMME FIVE! (OR TEN)

The second way to simplify your numbers is to round to the nearest five or ten dollars when preparing your Spending Plans. After you work with the same numbers over a period of time, you'll find they are easier to remember when they are rounded to significant digits. Let's look at some examples:

Cash to Burn

Isn't it easier to remember you need $70, $100, or $120 every week rather than $71, $132, or $127? The extra level of precision gained by detailing to the exact dollar is not worth the added difficulty in remembering the number. This is an amount you need to remember since you use it every week. Your ATM system helps you here since you can only withdraw in even amounts of tens and twenties.

Flexible Money

This is perhaps the most important number to simplify since you will need to know this number every month, and it will *change* every month. After creating your Actual Spending

Plan, suppose you come up with Flexible Money of $153. Round down to $150. If the number is $179, round up to $180. As you spend against that number, you can either keep a mental tally of what's left (risky) or track it on a Post-it™ note on your check register. I prefer to play it safe and use the Post-it™ note method.

One last point—be sure you don't have big problems making small changes when organizing your money!

Bella has no problem with big changes. Instead, she'd have a big problem with no change, especially with her money. No doubt about it, she wants a big change and she wants it in her wallet—right now!

Not the same kind of change, Bella, but you've got the idea.

SUMMARY

Get in the habit of simplifying your money numbers by rounding. You'll save time, reduce frustration, and easily follow your Spending Plans.

TAKE ACTION

- Calculate how much money you will earn during your lifetime if you work for thirty years at your current salary. Round to the nearest hundred thousand.

Chapter Seventeen

Planning with Unpredictable Income

> *There is only one success—to be able to spend your life in your own way.*
>
> —Christopher Morley

Does your work bring you a fluctuating and unpredictable paycheck, creating yet another wrinkle in your plans to keep the finances smooth? Perhaps you receive commissions that are high one month and low another. Or, you own a business and are subject to the ups and downs of the economy like all businesses. Do you receive cash tips daily and quickly spend the money without knowing how much it was and where it went? Perhaps it is difficult to predict *when* you will receive your income as well as how *much* it will be, which happens when providing consulting work. While you have the excitement of working independently, you also have the challenge of anticipating the right level of income to plan your spending correctly. How do you use your Spending Plan when your income is an unknown from month to month?

THE ANSWERS

There are two methods. The first is the Ebb and Flow method. It allows your level of spending to fluctuate up and down with the changes in your income. The second is the Steady State method, which gives you a constant level of spending regardless of the ups and downs of your income. You might want to start with the Ebb and Flow method and work toward the Steady State method if you are beginning a new job or career and are unsure what income to expect each month. Under the Ebb and Flow method, there is no way you can overspend your income without choosing to. (But you may have some lean months.) Under the Steady State method, you adjust your spending upward or downward only periodically to correct previous income estimates that may have resulted in over- or underspending.

EBB AND FLOW

Under this method you use the amount of money you received *last month* as the income for your Spending Plan *this month*. There is no guesswork because you don't *spend* it until you *have* it. Your Cash Cushion of one month's spending gets you started the first month. Here's how it works for Bella, who gets a commission check of varying amounts every other week, after deducting her taxes.

	Spending Plan Money	Income Received
MARCH		
Bella has saved a $1,500 Cash Cushion that she expects will last one month. She spends this in the first month while receiving commission payments of $1,250.	$1,500	$1,250

APRIL

Since she already has $1,250 $1,250 $1,400
in the bank, she uses this amount
as her new income figure. She is
motivated to earn more because she
wants to spend more next month. It
works, and she earns $1,400.

MAY

This month she spends the $1,400 $1,400 $1,700
she earned last month and doubles
her efforts to increase sales. WOW!
She earns $1,700 and can hardly
wait until next month to spend it.

JUNE

Happy days! She gets to spend $1,700 $1,650
$1,700 this month, and she loves
it. She is diligent in keeping her
sales work focused so she can enjoy
more months of fun spending *and*
begin saving for a trip to the tropics.
She earns $1,650 in June, which
she'll put in her Spending Plan for July.

When using the Ebb and Flow method, be sure you receive the money, or are certain to receive it, during the first month so you can count on it for next month's Spending Plan. Don't make a habit of counting on money not yet received, or you'll get ahead of yourself and spend next month's income now. Worse yet, you may count on and spend more money than you actually get.

STEADY STATE

This is for people who prefer not to let the ups and downs of their income affect their lifestyle and spending habits. It works best when you've been in a job long enough to have a realistic sense of how much income to expect for your work. To achieve Steady State, estimate a reasonable amount of income for a typical month. Be careful not to overestimate this figure. It's better to start with a conservative number and end with a happy surprise than to wind up in the red after your effort. Building good news into your system keeps your view of money positive!

Once you have a realistic income number, stick to it for a three-month period. Ignore minor fluctuations in your actual income. Get used to living on a steady amount of money regardless of temporary swings. At the end of the first three months, check your progress by calculating an average income based on your actual dollars received. If you have consistently brought in more than your estimate and want to increase the income number in your Spending Plan, do so gradually over the next several three-month reviews. If you have consistently fallen short, scale back your Spending Plan while maintaining your income goals. If the actual average comes close to your predictions, congratulate yourself and continue using the same income estimate for the next three months. When you are comfortable with this method, you may want to check your estimates less often, perhaps every six months, so as not to vary your lifestyle too much. After all, you are pursuing the Steady State!

The Steady State method is riskier than the Ebb and Flow method since you are spending money you may not earn. You can reduce this risk by safely estimating your income lower than you expect. Any positive differences accumulate as savings and can be used for anything you want.

Hint: To simplify the Steady State method, deposit your paychecks into your savings account as they are received. Each month, transfer the amount of Spending Plan Income to your checking account. This way you make one clean transaction for income and any surplus stays in savings.

WHICH ONE?

Neither method is better than the other, so pick the one that best matches your style of living and spending. Some people find they want to count on a steady amount; fluctuations don't appeal to them. They are confident they will earn enough money to support their own spending level. These people select the Steady State method. Others want to splurge after achieving a big month and live free from the risk of ever going in the red. They select the Ebb and Flow method. Pick one, or try both, then stick with the method that works best for you.

THE CASH CUSHION

Both methods require you to start with a Cash Cushion, which is always a necessity when you don't get paid at regular intervals. Your Cash Cushion will need to be one month's level of spending, provided you expect to get paid *at least* monthly. If you are paid less often, you need a higher Cash Cushion available to accommodate long spending stretches without income. If you haven't already saved the right amount for your Cash Cushion, make it an Action Item and do it.

A TIP ON TIPS

If you receive cash tips, estimate your weekly amount. Compare this to your Cash-to-Burn amount. Accumulate your actual cash tips one week and use this for next week's Cash-to-Burn money instead of visiting your ATM. If you collect *more* than your Cash to Burn during the week, make a trip to the bank and deposit the extra tips. If you receive *less*, withdraw the difference when you visit the bank. This way you are smoothing the effect of tips on your overall income. When you can estimate a reliable amount of tips to expect, subtract your Cash-to-Burn amount. Include a positive difference as Tip *Income* on your Spending Plan and a negative one as an *expense* under Cash to Burn.

Since Bella's average commission over the last four months is $1,500, she puts that in her TOTAL INCOME box even though she has every intention of working hard to increase it, possibly moonlighting for a while. She'd rather be conservative and have good news than be overly optimistic and have to cut back.

SUMMARY

The key to success with unpredictables is to turn them into predictables. A time lag does it. Delay listing an unpredictable amount on your Spending Plan until you've received the money. Then you know you've got it and you know the amount. If you receive $120 from a garage sale in July, include it in August's Spending Plan. This works with commissions, profit sharing, tips, bonuses, and all miscellaneous income (garage sales, gifts, odd jobs, etc.).

TAKE ACTION

- Decide which income method you like best.

- Save a sufficient Cash Cushion.

- If you receive cash tips, estimate a weekly amount. Save one week of tips to use for your Cash to Burn the following week.

Chapter Eighteen

Treat Your Taxes as a Bonus

> *A good income cures most ills.*
> —Jewish folk saying
>
> *Except taxes.*
> —Karen Brigham

There's a lot to know about taxes. The good news is you don't need to know much right now to meet your goals. What you need to focus on are two things: learning how to enjoy tax time, and learning how to roughly calculate the correct amount of money to pay our Uncle throughout the year. The two objectives are linked together; you accomplish the first by accomplishing the second. (Are they backward?) Let's take a look.

MISSION IMPOSSIBLE?

Enjoy tax time? Who in their right mind ever enjoys that three-and-a-half-month period that starts the first day of the beautiful new year and ends on that date everyone dreads—April 15?! All those forms and frustration? The anxiety and suspense leading up to that terrible moment when you find out you might actually have to *pay additional money* (Oh no! Anything but that, please! There must be a mistake—check it again!) If you've lived through the unpleasant surprise of owing money on April 15, you know it's nothing you want to repeat.

How about this instead? You look forward to getting your W-2 form in the mail. Ah, finally you can complete your tax returns, double-check them, and rapidly mail them in. You anticipate the last step—how much money will you get back this year? You hurry to get your returns in early, knowing they will be processed quickly and you'll get that fat refund check faster. You enjoy the waiting time though, thinking about what to do with the money. Such a big chunk of cash! It's fun to come up with possibilities. A little vacation? That nice dining room set? Squirrel away some money for the down payment on that 4WD urban assault vehicle? Pay off the last credit card so you'll be totally debt free and able to go full throttle on your *Saving Habit?* So many wonderful possibilities—how to decide? What a dilemma!

STRATEGIZE

What's the difference between the two scenarios? Using different strategies from the start. The first leaves everything fairly well to chance, and you may or may not regret it. The second requires a little planning to calculate a withholding amount so you *receive a refund.* What? Let's repeat that— *plan to receive a refund.* Yes, I know this is contrary to what you may have heard in other financial books or from other financial experts. Their theory goes like this: Give Uncle Sam as little as you can get away with during the year so his money earns interest in *your* account, before going to the government's pockets.

This is a fine theory, and it can work *if you follow it.* Most people don't. Many don't want to calculate the exact amount they will owe the government. The skills required to do this may be more than they want to learn now. Some don't put the money safely away in a savings account to happily surrender to the IRS at tax time. Not only is there no interest earned on Uncle Sam's money, there is no money either! So why not make a positive experience out of the annual event instead of trying to gain a small amount of interest and forking over a big check?

After a couple years of enjoying the experience of getting refund checks, your attitude toward April 15 will be positive. At that point, you may be interested in learning more and can change your strategy if you like. Right now, I still plan for a refund even though I am capable of following the more commonly prescribed strategy. Getting the extra money is like getting a present once a year. The extra interest doesn't give me nearly the excitement of knowing I'll receive a large lump of money once a year.

Once you accept the strategy of aiming for a refund, it is less important to know how to calculate your withholdings exactly to the penny. It's perfectly acceptable to err on the side of being too high. As a matter of fact, it's desirable. To estimate the total amount to contribute to the government, get your returns from last year (state and federal) and a recent pay stub. You may also need some information from your payroll department, which will be easy for them to provide.

QUICK AND DIRTY—THE GUESSWORK METHOD

Did you receive a refund from your taxes last year or did you end up paying more? If you paid additional taxes on April 15, you want to *decrease* the number of withholding allowances on your W-4 form, which is on file in the payroll department of your company. Claiming zero withholding allowances tells your employer to take out *more* taxes than claiming five.

Remember, if you err on the side of withholding too much money you'll be that much happier at the end of the year. Whatever is taken out that the government is not entitled to keep comes back to you. Paying more throughout the year does not mean it's gone for good. Your payroll department will give you the information you need to estimate the new number of allowances to claim. Or simply claim one or two less allowances than you did last year until you get a substantial refund.

TO BE EXACT

If you want to be more precise, and all tax events in your life are the same this year as last year, you can follow this example. Let's say you paid $1,000 extra in taxes last year over and above what was withheld, and you want to receive a refund of $2,000 this year. You'll need to withhold approximately $3,000 *more* this year, or close to it. If you are paid monthly, this will amount to withholding $250 *more* per paycheck ($3,000 divided by twelve). If you are paid semimonthly (twice a month) this will be $125 more per paycheck ($3,000 divided by twenty-four). And if you are paid biweekly (every other week) you'll need to take out $115 more per paycheck ($3,000 divided by twenty-six). Calculate the additional amount and add it to the amount that is being deducted now with the current number of allowances you are claiming. This gives you the total you wish to have deducted *per paycheck*. (You need to do this for both state and federal taxes.)

Your payroll department will give you the number of allowances to claim for the new amount you want withheld. Or, you can simply write the additional amount *per paycheck* on your W-4 form in the box labeled "Additional amount, if any, you want deducted from each pay." This way your basic withholding amount adjusts automatically when you receive a raise and the additional amount is deducted as well.

OH NO YOU DON'T

You may be thinking, "Take money out! More money I don't get? No thank you, I need every penny!" In the short term, you may need it. Come the end of the year you'll need it for taxes because you'll still owe the same amount whether or not it is deducted throughout the year. You can either avoid the issue all year and set yourself up for an unpleasant surprise around the middle of April, or you can *plan* to handle this expense in a more positive, proactive way. I'm in favor of proactive planning and positive results. Like a few other things in life, your tax expense doesn't go away if you choose not to look at it or think about it throughout the year. Of course you can *lower* your overall expense by looking closely at all the loopholes available to you and applying them as prescribed by your tax preparer. This affects the amount you *owe*, not the amount *withheld* throughout the year.

TRY THIS

A good time to make this change is when you get a raise. Your taxes will change then anyway since it is generally true that the more you make the more they take. To accommodate this, you may want to decrease your withholding allowances by one or two each time you get a raise until you find the number that gives you a nice refund. At first it will seem like you haven't gotten much of a raise, but you'll appreciate it at the end of the year when a large sum of money comes your way. This way you move *gradually* toward a larger and larger refund at the end of each year, and give your lifestyle time to adjust to the change in take-home pay.

WATCH OUT

Be on the alert for events in your life that increase your tax bill so you can change your withholdings *when* the event happens (don't wait until the end of the year). Here's a list of some basic life events that affect your taxes:

Event	Effect on Your Tax Bite
Marriage to a nonworking spouse	Decrease
Marriage to a working spouse	Increase or Decrease
Birth of children	Decrease
Purchase of first home	Decrease
Increase in salary	Increase
Divorce of a nonworking spouse	Increase
Alimony payments—Paid	Decrease
Alimony payments—Received	Increase
Child support payments—Paid	No effect
Child support payments—Received	No effect

You can either determine for yourself how these events affect your tax picture or call the person who prepares your return. Remember not to ignore these events. As your financial prosperity increases, you will learn more about our tax laws *out of necessity*. You cannot remain in the dark about such a large expense in your life. For now, you need to accomplish more important goals to get you to that point of greater wealth.

SOCIAL WHAT?

A word about another major expense—Social Security tax. Unlike income taxes, there is nothing you can do to lower or avoid these payments. Your employer is required by law to withhold the prescribed amount from each of your checks until you've reached the maximum. I recommend you periodically (every three years) request a "Personal Earnings and Benefits Statement" from the Social Security Administration. (To get this you file a Form 7004. The SSA will send this to you if you call them at 1-800-772-1213 or use their web site, ssa.gov.) The important information supplied by the Earnings Statement is how much Social Security tax is on record as being contributed by you. Check the numbers supplied by them with the amount on your W-2 form for each year (filed with your copy of your tax return). Any discrepancy is better caught now than thirty years from now when you are ready to retire and receive benefits.

NO REGRETS

Once you have taken all steps to legally reduce your taxes, try to think positively about this expense. Think of this payment in terms of the benefits and lifestyle you are afforded by our government. There must be *some things* you enjoy, even if you take them for granted. Think of your taxes as dues to one of the best country clubs in the world—aren't you glad to be a member? It is useless to consider this an optional expense and focus on how much more you'd have if you didn't have to pay taxes. Better to look at what you *have left* and use your Spending Plan to get the most out of it!

Bella got a refund last year and hasn't changed her W-4 form. Since the tax events in her life haven't changed, she's headed for a refund again this year.

Good going, Bella!

SUMMARY

Turn tax time into a holiday by planning for a refund. Then take a vacation with the money you get back!

TAKE ACTION

- Find your tax returns from last year. Did you make a payment or get a refund? If you paid, write down your total taxes.

- Go to your payroll department and find out how many allowances you need to claim to get $1,000 back. Change your W-4 form. Or—

- Ask your tax preparer to tell you how many allowances to claim on your W-4 form to get $1,000 back, then change it.

- Call 1-800-772-1213 and order a Form 7004. File Form 7004 to receive your Personal Earnings and Benefits Statement. Check the amount of Social Security tax paid by you on the statement with the amounts on your W-2 forms for the same years.

Chapter Nineteen

The Benefits of Giving Your Money Away

A man gives little when he gives much with a frown;
he gives much when he gives little with a smile.

—Jewish folk saying

Many questions arise around the personal choice of contributing money to worthy organizations. How much? How often? Which organizations? When to start? And certainly, why? Answers are abundant in prosperity literature and with spiritual leaders. The prosperity books listed in Appendix A offer explanations on the subject.

I used to feel awkward when approached for contributions. One side of me wanted to be generous, another side wanted to keep the money for myself. A big part of me resented whoever was raising the confusion. I gave only small amounts, if anything.

THE EXPERIMENT

To put an end to the internal struggle once and for all, I did an experiment. The minister of my church made a convincing case for tithing, or donating 10% of my income. (Gross, pre-tax income.) I decided to try tithing only to find out what would happen, with no other expectations. *Curiosity* compelled me more than *generosity*. I promised myself if I didn't like the results I would stop the experiment. Few people knew

I was trying this. The ones who did thought it was out of character for me and they were probably right.

THE RESULTS

The results are in. Giving money gives me satisfaction. I enjoy helping others by supporting organizations that could not exist without contributions. I've benefited during my life from non-profit organizations. Now I can help them by giving generously back. Giving freely feels strong, successful, and prosperous. The bottom line of my experiment is this: Contributing money to organizations that are important to me brings benefits I value more than keeping or spending the same money.

NO STRINGS ATTACHED

Your *intention* when giving is critical. Focus on supporting a cause that's important to you and that relies on donations. Make sure you are externally focused instead of self-focused. You'll read stories about people who gave away 10% of their income and found large sums of money immediately coming back to them. This may happen, but it should not be the *reason* you give. Expect your highest return to be how you feel about yourself instead of a bigger bank account. Do not confuse donating with investing.

PLANNING TO GIVE

It's easy to put a line for Giving in your Spending Plan each month. If you want to give away a certain percentage of your income, but cannot work the amount immediately into your Spending Plan, make it another goal. Instead of giving the full 10% right away, work up to it over a year's time, giving 3%, 5%, 7%, 9%, then the full 10%.

If you give large amounts to one organization such as a church, think about making monthly payments instead of weekly ones. Organizations accept your donation whenever it's convenient for you, and it's easier to deal with one check each month than four or five. At the end of the year, you have only twelve amounts to round up for your taxes instead of fifty-two. Quite a difference!

Be warned, many organizations rely on mass mailings to raise funds and will keep you on their list perpetually after you donate a significant amount or if you contribute when they send you a request. This may be either a convenience or an annoyance to you. However, do not let it deter you from giving to a worthy cause. Create a Charity Folder for the requests you want to respond to. Pull out the folder when you do your Money Mechanics and want to give. If you no longer wish to receive mail, write and tell them.

Bella's been generous longer than I have; she already includes donations to her church in her Spending Plan. She's not so sure about giving 10% though—that's a lot higher than she's comfortable with. She's surprised to see I recommend it and wonders if I really follow my own recommendations—especially this one.

OK, Bella, your hunch is right—I don't follow *all* my recommendations *all the time.* It's true, I sometimes use my credit card when it's not an emergency. Once in a while you might catch me with extra Cash to Burn in my pocket. And there are times when I come close to saying "It's not in my budg——." But this one I'm good for. Yes, 10%. I know, Bella, hard to believe, but it's true.

SUMMARY

If you're involved with an organization that inspires you to give, become a financial scientist and put your generosity to the test!

TAKE ACTION

- Take a poll among your rich friends. Ask if they make large donations and find out why or why not.

Chapter Twenty
Money without Madness for Couples

The man who marries for money earns it.

—Jewish folk saying

The *Money Without Madness System* works as well for couples as it does for single people. First decide how certain items on the Spending Plan will be divvied up—whether they are *shared* items or *separate*. Since each marriage (or relationship) has different preferences and financial circumstances, this will vary from couple to couple. Some couples keep all their money together in one pool, others keep it separate. There are variations in between, and preferences change as circumstances and relationships change. Let's take a look at several couples and see how they use their Spending Plans together.

YOUR MONEY IS MY MONEY IS OUR MONEY

Kathy and Richard share everything in their marriage so it is natural for them to pool their finances. They have joint checking and savings accounts. Kathy and Richard both have incomes and their paychecks are automatically deposited in their joint checking account. Kathy is the Money Manager. She uses the Spending Plan for the family finances.

She lists her income and Richard's in the income section of the Spending Plan. For Cash to Burn, she and Richard agree she needs $80 a week while he'll take $120 because he buys the food each week. They each get their own cash from the ATM. Kathy pays the monthly bills when she does the Money Mechanics. Then she lists the items she wants to buy from their Flexible Money. She completes the amounts they wish to pay on their credit cards and the amount of money to transfer to savings.

She and Richard review last month's Spending Plan and the Spending Plan for the upcoming month together. Richard considerately lets her know of any Flexible Money he will need, either specific or nonspecific. If there are problems, they reach solutions together and make reasonable adjustments. Taking time each month to go over their finances keeps them both aware and involved, and is a good way for them to stay on track with their mutually agreed upon goals. A perfect couple in many ways, they never fight except when Richard wants to get in on the fun of doing the Money Mechanics. Kathy stubbornly refuses to give it up, which is always good for at least one well-mannered tête-à-tête.

YOUR MONEY IS YOUR MONEY, MY MONEY IS MY MONEY

Noah and Sara prefer to keep finances out of the marital arena. They have different spending styles and different financial goals. Noah wants to use Money Mechanics and Spending Plans to achieve his goals and Sara thinks it's unnecessary. They split all shared expenses down the middle. Each pays half when they buy groceries together, and they alternate picking up the tab for entertainment. They understand neither one is responsible for half an expense unless that person has agreed to the purchase in advance. Separate expenses are paid for separately. Sara spends her money on high-tech toys, and Noah enjoys buying accoutrements for his motocross hobby.

Since Noah uses Money Mechanics for his own finances, it is easy for him to pay the joint bills and get one check from Sara for her half. This way he knows it's done and he sleeps better. Sara and Noah have separate credit cards and savings accounts. Noah has more aggressive savings goals than Sara because he wants to start a business. Sara is working on paying off her credit cards as she puts herself through school for a degree in computer science.

YOUR MONEY, MY MONEY, AND OUR MONEY

Barry and Genoa identify most of their expenses as shared. They set up a joint account called the Household account in addition to their own separate accounts. Their paychecks are each deposited into their own accounts. At the end of the month, Barry does the couple's Money Mechanics. The Spending Plan covers only the Household account so each partner takes care of their own individual expenses separately. Barry totals the expenses from the Household Spending Plan, and divides it in half. Both he and Genoa then write a check from their individual accounts to the Household account. These checks go into the Spending Plan on the INCOME line.

The expenses they agree are covered by Household money include: rent, utilities, phone, food, family health club dues, medical bills, and children's expenses. They have a credit card for Household purchases such as furniture, small household items, family outings, etc. This is paid in full out of the Household account each month. Each person takes his or her Cash to Burn out of the Household account, so those amounts are reflected on the Cash line. Barry takes $80 a week and Genoa takes $120 since she spends more cash on the kids. If Barry runs short, Genoa usually has some cash to give him. Since the couple has a joint savings goal, that payment is included on the Spending Plan and therefore in the total Barry divides in two.

From their individual money each partner covers their own car payment and related insurance and maintenance costs, as well as anything that is personal such as clothing. They are free to manage that money, spending or saving it as they want without providing an explanation to their partner. This gives them a flexibility and independence they both enjoy. Genoa has her own credit card she uses whenever she travels. Barry makes his child support payments out of his personal account.

A TALKING TOOL

The Spending Plan is useful as a discussion tool to decide which items you want to combine and which you want to keep separate. Start at the top with Income.

Income can be used as the basis for dividing expenses if you don't think a 50/50 split is fair. This is most common when there is a large discrepancy between the amount of money two people make. The partner making more money can afford to contribute more, leaving the partner who makes less with a lower payment and some money left for themselves. The expenses are split according to the percentage of income each person contributes to the total. For example:

	Income	*Percent of Total*
Husband	$24,000	40%
Wife	$36,000	60%
	$60,000	100%

In this example, all shared expenses will be split so Husband pays 40% of them and Wife pays 60%. When either income changes, the percentages are recalculated.

Next, talk about your Cash to Burn. How much does each person need and what items will the money cover? Do you want it to come out of a shared account or to be covered separately? What happens when one person runs out and the other doesn't? Should one have more than the other or should it be equal?

Many of the items in the CHECKS section (housing, phone, utilities) will be used together—do you want them to be paid jointly? This is where you can apply the percentages calculated above if you want. Some couples prefer to keep the split 50/50 on the basis that each are equal partners in the relationship. It's up to you.

FLEXIBLE DISCUSSIONS

Some expenses falling into the Flexible Money category are usually discussed between two people anyway. These include major purchases, emergencies, child-related expenses, items for the home, etc. In a general discussion you can decide which items will be jointly covered and which ones your partner may choose not to share. New items that do not neatly fall into the categories you previously agreed upon will always appear. These can be discussed as they come up.

Many people want some Flexible Money to spend freely without guilt. This may be especially true in a marriage or relationship, since someone else is looking over your spending choices. It's one thing to answer to yourself at the end of the month—and another to answer to your lifelong partner. If either of you need this freedom, be sure to include an unidentified chunk of money in the Spending Plan for yourselves. You can first see how it fits on paper, and make adjustments, if necessary, to accommodate this priority.

When you talk about the last two items—Debt and Savings—you are really opening up a discussion about your goals, shared and separate. Do you have debt you want to pay back separately, or is it shared debt to be paid off together? How quickly? Savings can be mutual or separate as well. What are your goals toward establishing a team *Saving Habit?* Once you decide what is shared and what is kept separate, you can apply the principles in the next chapter, *Twelve Steps to Financial Freedom,* to your shared goals the same as you do to your individual goals.

WHO MANAGES THE MONEY?

One of you will be the Money Manager for the shared money. This is the person who will do the Money Mechanics every month. The Money Manager needs to be *interested* in taking on the work, good with details and organization, and free of judgment toward spending styles different from his or her own. The purpose of managing the shared money is to control the money, not the partner. Although the Money Manager does the work, both partners are still responsible for carrying out their end of the agreement as best they can. The other partner may be interested in seeing the monthly Spending Plan and providing input for their own Flexible Money. Switching roles after six months or a year is a good idea. It gives both partners an understanding and appreciation of the process, and the ability to handle it themselves if they ever need to.

FIGHTS ABOUT MONEY THAT ARE NOT ABOUT MONEY

Money is a hot topic in some marriages. Yet, if two people are reasonable and willing to work out a solution, one is always available. When nothing is acceptable to either partner, it's likely that money is not the real issue of disagreement. If you suspect this to be true, check it out with your partner. If other issues are involved, get another book.

While Bella looks forward to meeting her financial goals herself and being independent as long as she wants to, she also loves the idea of sharing her goals with the right man, working to reach them *together.* How nice to have two incomes instead of one. It'll be fun to talk once a month about their progress and decide together how to spend their money. Bella is sure there will be no fights about money because she and her man will cozy up and communicate about everything.

SUMMARY

Mixed money marriages are the norm these days, giving couples more choices about who owns the money and who manages the money. If you haven't found what works best for you, throw out the standard notions and try some new ways of handling the money in your relationship!

TAKE ACTION

- Ask some couples you know how they handle money together and how well it works.

- Talk to your partner about the current division of expenses to see if he or she wants to make any changes.

Part Four ⌒

Change the Way You Think About Money

Let's give our left brains a break and our right brains some equal time. Success with money requires more from us than crunching numbers and juggling bottom lines. Each person, couple, or family has their own unique goals for their money. To reach these goals, we need to establish good money habits firmly in our lives. To help you establish those habits, the *Money Without Madness* System gives you a simple checklist to keep you focused. It's foolproof if you follow it!

But total success with money requires more. We need to put some soul into our pocketbooks, and the way we do that is through our attitude. Developing a new attitude toward our money gives us the instant benefits of feeling good about our money and stopping any money stress we have.

Do you need to change your spending habits to start saving more money or paying down your credit card debt? You've come to the right section! The key here is to substitute and delay rather than to deny yourself anything. But that's not all. What do you say when spending temptations sneak up on you and why are the words you use important?

You'll find out how this fits together in the following section as we cover the right brain tactics of using new words to create a new attitude. Not only is this fun—it's free! So relax and learn how to give yourself a new money attitude.

Chapter Twenty-One

Twelve Steps to Financial Freedom

Life is not about goals, it's about growth.

—Student of *A Course in Miracles*

We've all heard by now—setting and reaching goals is important if you intend to get what you want in life. But when it comes to money, especially when we *first* look at this area of our lives, many of us are confused by the number of goals we should have and which ones come first. Reduce debt or save? Enjoy life now or plan for retirement? Spend as though you *already* have more money or spend conservatively so you *will* have more? Everyone tells us to set goals, but where do we start? The whole thing becomes complicated and confusing. It's easy to get discouraged and give up.

GOOD HABITS = GROWTH

Let's simplify. Before you tackle any *major financial goals,* you need to grow. To grow, you need to add *three key money habits* to your life:

1. *Manage your money monthly.*

2. *Gain credit card freedom.*

3. *Start saving now.*

The *mechanics* of these habits were discussed in previous chapters. Now, we'll talk about the *process* of making them part of your life. You need to learn them, live them, and continue using them to progress through your *major financial goals*. The three key money habits are not ends to achieve then forget. They are *habits* to add to the way you live your life. Living these habits is a *prerequisite* for success with future goals.

A PATH

Below is a recommended path, made up of twelve specific and successive steps, to ease you out of your current situation and into living the three key money habits. Each of these twelve steps is a goal in itself. You aim for it, accomplish it, then move on. All you do is go down the list, check off the goals as you accomplish them, and achieve the remaining ones in the order presented. Working with your Spending Plan every month and doing your Money Mechanics helps you complete each step. It's simple, and you'll feel good knowing what you've accomplished, what the next step is, and what you're working toward.

The Twelve Steps to Financial Freedom

❏ 1. Get an income.

❏ 2. Complete your first Actual Spending Plan.

❏ 3. Do your Money Mechanics every month.

❏ 4. Close *all* your store charge accounts to future charges.

(Do your Money Mechanics every month!)

❏ 5. Stop charging on *all* other credit cards except to make emergency payments and occasional convenience purchases.

❏ 6. Make at least the *minimum* payments on all credit card debt (more if you can).

(Do your Money Mechanics every month!)

❏ 7. *Follow* your Spending Plan.

❏ 8. Save 5% of your take-home income every month.

❏ 9. Pay off *all* credit card debt. Close all but two major credit cards.

(Do your Money Mechanics every month!)

❏ 10. Save 7% of your take-home income every month.

❏ 11. Save 10% of your take-home income every month.

(Do your Money Mechanics every month!)

❏ 12. Indulge yourself in something you really want. You deserve it!

EASY DOES IT

Don't expect to whip through this list in a few quick months. It could easily take years to complete. I was stuck on Number 7 (Follow your Spending Plan) for two years. Sometimes I still have trouble with it. For many people *The Twelve Steps to Financial Freedom* might realistically be a five-year plan. The right time frame for you depends on your levels of income, spending, and debt, and your sense of urgency.

I encourage you to make easy, gradual changes so you know they are real, rather than temporary changes sparked by fleeting motivation. For example, when you get to Number 4 (Close *all* store charge accounts to future charges), live with it for a while before moving on to Number 5 (Stop charging on *all* other credit cards). If you are using store charge cards now, you need time to make that change *before* taking care of the other credit cards in your life. If you try to do too much too fast, you won't sustain your progress.

CELEBRATE, CELEBRATE

Reward yourself after you accomplish each step. It's important to recognize progress and celebrate each positive change in your life. Rewarding yourself prevents backsliding and helps you focus on the next goal. If your accomplishment is a joint effort, involve your partner in the celebration, too.

Make sure the reward is consistent with the rest of your money goals. Give meaning to something ordinary: a bubble bath, dinner at home with flowers and candles, a manicure or pedicure (men too), an evening or day free to do whatever you want, a new book or magazine. More important than spending a lot of money is making something symbolize your achievement. Tell yourself, "As soon as I close all my store charge accounts I'm headed to the beach to celebrate my new progress," and watch how you enjoy working toward that goal.

BY THE WAY . . .

The reason I recommend starting your *Saving Habit* before paying off all your credit card debt is simple. It's to build the Safety Fund we talked about. You could lose your source of income at any point on this path. If you are then without money to live on because you conscientiously paid off your debts, your creditors will be happier than you. Pay yourself first. If you find yourself without an income, remember to return to Number 1 (Get an income) until it is accomplished. Put all other steps on hold except Number 3 (Do your Money Mechanics every month). Maintaining this habit helps you through unemployment by reducing stress about managing the money you are drawing from your Safety Fund.

THE MORE FORMULA

You may notice *The Twelve Steps to Financial Freedom* tell you *what* to do—they don't tell you *how* to do it. How you accomplish these steps depends on the amount of money you have left each month to put toward your goals. To create more money in your life you must do one of two things: Bring more money in or let less money out. There are only two components to the equation. You may work on both areas at once and turbo-charge your efforts, but you must take action and make changes in at least *one* of these two places or *nothing will change.*

To increase your income you may improve your current earning potential, supplement it with a second income, or change careers. What is right for you depends on other values in your life: your beliefs about your work purpose and the prosperity available to you, the importance of material items to your happiness, your level of confidence, and your comfort with risk. Understanding these beliefs may take some meaningful soul-searching. Many books are available to help you. I've listed some I like in Appendix A at the back of this book. Read them for guidance on your journey to greater prosperity.

THE COMPLETE SOLUTION

If you choose to pursue a higher income, do it *in conjunction* with your progress on *The Twelve Steps to Financial Freedom.* Following the steps to develop and keep good money habits is *not optional.* Many folks attract more incoming cash only to find the extra money slips away. They didn't use a management tool such as the Spending Plan in conjunction with their goals. Your Spending Plan keeps you motivated and stretches every new dollar further toward your goals. Successfully bringing in more money is only half the solution. Working with the money you bring in and using it to reach your goals is the complete answer.

Bella's got Cancun written at the bottom of her *Twelve Steps to Financial Freedom*. She's checked off Number 1 and Number 2. Tomorrow she's going to the department store and close her account so she can check off Number 4. All right, this is great! She'll move through this list in no time—bubble baths, manicures, and pedicures all part of the deal, too!

SUMMARY

Before proceeding with fancy investments, crafty tax strategies, and meaningful retirement goals, you need to acquire the three key money habits. Move through *The Twelve Steps to Financial Freedom* at a pace that's comfortable for you. Before you know it, you'll find yourself living the three key money habits and attracting more money into your life. Remember, there is no level of income to which your spending cannot rise. Keep your cash flow organized and put it toward your goals.

1. *Manage your money monthly.*

2. *Gain credit card freedom.*

3. *Start saving now.*

TAKE ACTION

- Copy *The Twelve Steps to Financial Freedom* list at the back of the book and check off any you've already accomplished.

- Determine your rewards for achieving the first three steps. Write them next to the steps.

- Think about a major financial goal to tackle once you've completed *The Twelve Steps to Financial Freedom*. Write it at the end of the list.

- Select a prosperity book from Appendix A at the end of the book and read it.

Chapter Twenty Two

Simplify Your Life to Maximize Your Good Fortune

He who knows he has enough is rich.

—Tao Te Ching

Many people in the United States are shifting away from life on the fast track, away from acquiring more and more material things. They are re-evaluating the priorities in their lives and changing their financial goals to accommodate new values. And why not? Americans have been in an acquisition mode—funded by debt—for several decades. People tire of doing the same thing over and over. It's natural now to seek quiet retreat and change our values—to simplify our lifestyles.

REST EASY

Financial simplification brings both financial and nonfinancial rewards. You struggle when you're spending more than you're making. You feel it every day with every purchase. It isn't pleasant—it's exhausting. It's not natural to push and push, never resting. It's natural to expand and relax, extend and retreat, grow and rest. Life doesn't naturally follow a perfectly straight line in an upward path, so why should we? Life alternates between growth spurts and quiet rests.

TAKE A BREATHER

Are you able to meet your savings and debt reduction goals with the money currently available to you? Or do you need to change your inflow or outflow of funds? Is 10% of your take-home pay available for Flexible Money? Can you count on receiving a tax refund at the end of the year? Are you able to live off your current income without further increasing your credit card debt? Can you comfortably save 10% of your income?

If you need to make some changes to improve any of these situations, consider shifting to a Better Basics lifestyle. It's a positive step you can take immediately. How long you keep this change depends on the goals you want to accomplish and the time you want it to take. View it as a healthy return to some basic, simpler things in life—a time to slow your lifestyle down a notch (in the materialistic sense).

ENOUGH IS ENOUGH

Simplifying your finances means simplifying your life. I've been through this a few times so I know it can be done creatively and enjoyably. Sound crazy? Give it a try. Here are some things that work for me along with those that don't. After you read them, make your own list, matching your situation to your own preferences in life.

For a Better Basics Lifestyle I Choose To:

- Share good meals with good friends at home instead of meeting at a restaurant.

- Make friends with the local library and read on. . . .

- Beat a path to the health club. *You don't need big bucks for big biceps.*

- Drive safely to avoid $186 tickets, traffic school, and doubling the cost of my auto insurance.

- Drive (safely) instead of fly (airplanes)? *Yes, for short trips.*

- Camp instead of stay home? *Sure, answer the call of the wild.*

- Write instead of call. *Saves a dying art as well as $$$s.*

- Apply old-fashioned elbow grease (my own) instead of wheeling through the all-cloth super car wash? *Absolutely.*

- Delay car maintenance? *Never again. Too costly in the long run.*

- Make good use of the VCR instead of the local movie house. *This has built-in advantages for a closer evening anyway.*

- Take back row seats at the theater? *No. The ballet? Maybe. The symphony? Definitely! The opera? Pass.*

- Shop at discount drugstores and outlet clothing stores? *I'm thinking about it.*

- Accept hand-me-down clothes from friends? *Absolutely—I have some classy friends.*

- Frequent garage sales? *Infrequently.*

- Use drugstore makeup instead of department store cosmetics. *Sorry, Bella.*

- Buy L'Eggs® mail-order seconds for my second-to-none gams.

- Repair shoes instead of replacing them? *Gimme some sole!*

- Hand pick wild flowers for a mason jar arrangement? *Naturally.*

- Squabble over the division of the dinner tab? *Never. (Poor taste!)*

- Take a doggie bag home from the restaurant? *Yes, wolf it down tomorrow.*

- Think twice about flying cross-country to see a favorite relative? *No. Check the Internet for discount airline tickets? Most definitely.*

- That divine suede jacket for $600? *Gotta pass. An excellent duplicate for $200? I'll take it!*

- Lower my 10% church donation? *Gotta confess, it crossed my mind. Having decided to stick with it, I give quickly and enjoy giving.*

NO CHEAP SHOTS

Understand, no one's recruiting for the How Cheap Can I Be? Club. My list includes things I am not willing to change because I enjoy them. I will continue to enjoy them regardless of my income level. Do the same! Change what you want, don't change anything you don't want. *Don't give up anything—* think about how to do it *differently* instead. Then *enjoy* doing it differently. The quality of your life does not have to come from the amount of money you spend. It comes from the enthusiasm you invest. Apply creativity and an open mind and find out what's really important to you.

I WANT TO!

In my own experience with a simpler, less-costly lifestyle, I found the *reason* for choosing the change to be all-important. Recently, I wanted to take time off to explore new interests instead of continuing my work with Silicon Valley start-up companies. Since this change was important to me, the cost mattered little. For me the key feature was that I *wanted* to do it.

I caution you against enduring this change as a necessary evil, an unpleasant means to an end. You may build regrets if it becomes a sentence of sacrifice. View it instead as an opportunity to challenge the current priorities in your life. It won't be a sacrifice if it is *your choice, your desire* for a better life. If the choice isn't self-motivated, you won't be content, and the changes won't last long. If you feel you're forced to reduce your spending, whether by unusual circumstances (loss of your job) or by someone else's influence on your life, you'll resent the lifestyle changes and return to your previous spending habits in no time flat.

Right, Bella?

Bella considers this chapter briefly. She's not crazy about staying home every night, taking in the evening sitcoms and munching on popcorn. She'd rather find a second job and get some extra money to pay off those credit cards faster. As she sees it, this has two advantages: She's bringing in more money to put toward that huge debt that built up when she wasn't looking, and a second job will keep her off the floors of better shopping malls, where her money disappears far too easily. That's Bella's idea of simplifying her life!

A fine idea, Bella. Have you thought about how you'll handle the spending opportunities on the floors of your own fine department store? You can hardly hope to stay away from shopping temptations when you work in the midst of them. Want some suggestions?

Bella is all ears.

Good—shop talk on goals, shoes, and thank you's coming right up!

SUMMARY

Focus on what you are _getting_ when you simplify your life, which is progress toward a financial goal. Think about your progress—think about _why_ you've elected to change your life. Think of the _gains_ you're making toward your goals rather than what you're missing. Attitude is all. Say to yourself "I'm working toward my goals and it feels good!" instead of "I am so poor, when will I ever get enough?"

TAKE ACTION

- Make a list of things you want to simplify in your life and those you don't. Spend the next three days adding to both lists.

- Ask friends for ideas that work for them.

⌐— Chapter Twenty-Three
Strategies for Resisting Budget Busters

And lead me not into temptation . . .

And lead me not into temptation . . .

And lead me not into temptation . . .

—The shopper's version of a popular prayer

Spending opportunities abound! Some are easy to resist— others are tempting. Have you had trouble resisting temptations in the past? Are you wondering how that will affect your new priorities and the spending choices you now want to make? Good question!

REPLACING BARGAINS WITH VALUES

Recognize that you are adding new financial values to your life. You are setting new goals and you need new spending behavior to support these goals. Every month you *plan* your spending to achieve your goals. This is a choice—*your* choice. Turning your plan into reality requires making that choice over and over again *during the month* as you face spending opportunities that are not in your Spending Plan. It is now important to use spending opportunities as opportunities to remind yourself what your new choices and priorities are, and at the same time, demonstrate *new* spending behavior.

NEW SHOP TALK

Making positive declarations about your financial goals and priorities rather than negative statements about yourself, your money, or the tempting item in front of you, is the key. Count on going through an adjustment period as your spending behavior shifts from *unplanned* to *planned* spending. Over time, your new spending behavior will become as automatic as you want it to be. Out with the negative, in with the positive! Let's see how . . .

FACE-TO-FACE—AND TEMPTED

Doesn't the world seem most full of convincing peddlers exactly at the time your Spending Plan calls for restraint? A shoe salesperson holds the cutest pair of $100 shoes in front of you and says, "How about these?" They *are* exactly the color you're looking for, exactly your size, and the heel is the right height. One thing stops you momentarily. You just finished your Spending Plan and it didn't include money for shoes. As a matter of fact, since you overspent last month (and what fun it was!), this is a tight month. There is only $70 left for your Flexible Money. You'd rather not spend it right away since you might need it later for something truly urgent (like dinner with that new employee in Customer Support). Meanwhile, here's the salesperson, the beautiful shoes, and you need an answer. Are you inclined to offer any of the following?

1. *No, I really don't like them.*
   (They're perfect and you love them.)

2. *I'm . . . not . . . sure.*
   (Can I get out of here before I cave in?)

3. *They're nice, but . . . too expensive.*
   (Are they really?)

4. *I don't want new shoes after all.*
   (You're dying for them.)

5. *I can't afford it. I don't have the money.*
   (The most dangerous of statements—read on.)

6. Or the concession, *Oh what the heck, I'll take them!*
   (Later you may feel tremendously guilty and possibly even return them—but probably not.)

What are these answers really saying? Are they insincere and easily abandoned to the persuasion of a good salesperson? As you walk away without your new shoes (if you do) will you feel deprived instead of good? Will you feel you've made *another* sacrifice because you *never have enough money?*

IN SEARCH OF THE TRUTH

Does this sound familiar? Let's look at the problems with the above replies, then abandon them for better ones. The strategies you learn here for face-to-face temptation work well in *all* tempting spending situations.

1. *No, I really don't like them.*

This feels uncomfortable because it is not true. In fact, you love everything about the shoes, so you might as well say it. The salesperson has done an excellent job selecting something so closely matching your taste. They deserve to know that as well.

2. *I'm . . . not . . . sure.*

Translation: "I want to be convinced to buy these. If you give me one good reason I will." Any good salesperson will offer plenty.

3. *They're nice, but . . . too expensive.*

Possibly, if the shoes are made cheaply and not worth the $100 price tag. If this is what you mean, you're on target. If they're fabulous quality and correctly priced but you are not willing to pay $100 for them, this is not an accurate response. The shoes and their price are not what's preventing you from opening your wallet. Guard against making statements convincing yourself that expensive merchandise is frivolous to purchase. Later on, when you have a plentiful pile of money, you may deny yourself the enjoyment of high-quality items because you told yourself so many times they were *too expensive*.

4. *I don't want new shoes after all.*

Useless. You know you want them. The salesperson knows you want them. Don't deny it—you only increase your frustration. Poor decisions come out of frustration. Don't let yourself off the hook without speaking the truth. If you really want these shoes, feel free to say so.

5. *I can't afford it. I don't have the money.*

Of all the responses, this may be the most common and the least helpful statement you can make. When you say this, you make a declaration *against* your own prosperity. *"I can't afford it."* You tell yourself and others you are living in perpetual sacrifice. It is not true. *"I don't have the money."* Yes, you do! You certainly *have* $100 to spend on something, even if it's the last $100 you have. What really is true is that you also have other things you *prefer* to spend that money on. You might very well prefer to spend it on food, rent, and other meaningful necessities, which is a reasonable choice. Don't say you "can't afford" something, or you "don't have the money," unless you *want* it to be true.

6. *Oh what the heck, I'll take them!*

If you decide you'd rather have the shoes than meet your Spending Plan this month, this is a great answer. Since you are certain of your priorities, this choice produces no guilt or afterthoughts. It is a valid decision—make it, and move forward. If this is *not* what you want, let's take a look at how to say what you want and get used to saying it.

NEW CHOICES

In these situations, you weigh two desires. You need to determine which one has a stronger place in meeting the overall goals that are important to your life. If you are certain you want to do everything possible to meet your Spending Plan, then make a choice against buying the shoes in favor of meeting your Spending Plan. That's it. You'd rather meet your Spending Plan than own that new pair of shoes. It's a choice, a preference, a declaration of your priorities, and *that* is what you tell yourself and the salesperson. Keeping this in mind, let's look at those responses again.

Instead of: *No, I really don't like them.*

Say: "They are perfect, but I don't want to spend $100 on shoes right now. Thank you for doing such a great job picking them out for me."

Instead of: *I'm . . . not . . . sure.*

Say: "I hadn't planned on buying shoes this month, but these are attractive. Let me think about it and I'll come back if I decide to take them."

Instead of: *They're nice, but . . . too expensive.*

Say: "They're fine shoes, and reasonably priced for such high quality. I don't want to spend $100 on shoes today, but thank you for showing them to me. I appreciate it."

Instead of: *I can't afford it. I don't have the money.*

Say: "Those are great shoes, but $100 shoes are not in my Spending Plan this month. Thanks for your help!"

Or: "I like those shoes, but I'd rather stick to my Spending Plan this month. I'll pass on them now and remember this store when I need shoes in the future. Thanks for showing them to me."

In the above answers you emphasize the *choice* you are making. Speak definitively, clearly, and with certainty to show you are comfortable with your choice. In tempting spending situations, think about your financial goals. After you make your decision, remind yourself you are now closer to meeting those goals than you were five minutes ago. Enjoy the satisfaction that comes from being in charge of the priorities in your life. It is easy to buy things when you are not used to saying no. Part of learning how to manage your money effectively means getting what you really want with your money. Instead of focusing on the shoes you didn't buy, think about your financial goals and why they are important to you.

MANY THANKS, ANYWAY!

Remember to thank the salesperson for helping you and to recognize a good product when offered. When you receive help from someone, they provide a service to you. While you may choose not to buy their product, it's nice to acknowledge their effort. Recognition of their product and sales skills, along with thanks, makes the personal interaction nicer for everyone.

ALONE—AND TEMPTED

What about the spending opportunities that come without the help of a skilled salesperson? It's tempting to get a quick dose of short-term satisfaction from buying something off the shelf *right now* or ordering from a catalog. Waiting for the less immediate, long-term advantages of reaching your debt reduction and savings goals can't compete, and the choice becomes more difficult because the benefits seem so far away.

They are. That's why you need to include some Flexible Money for truly spontaneous spending in your Spending Plan *each month*. Satisfy your immediate spending needs with that money. After you've spent it all and still find fun things to buy, put them on your Want List and wait until the beginning of next month. This is always less than thirty days away. Spending money *now* takes the edge off waiting to reach long-term goals. Balance is the key. You reach your long-term goals *and* satisfy your immediate spending desires when you balance your spending between these goals each month.

When you need to wait, tell *yourself* the same things you told the salesperson in the above situation. These are not just responses to another person, but declarations to yourself about your new preferences and choices in life. While fondling a $100 fountain pen so smooth it writes your memoirs automatically, say to yourself, "I *love* this pen, but it's important to me to *follow* my Spending Plan so I can start a **Saving Habit**. I *prefer* to buy this pen next month after I see how it fits into my Spending Plan." Go home and put the pen and its price on your Want List.

Every time you're tempted, use all the responses you would if you were face-to-face with a great salesperson, even when you're not. Start with the words, *I prefer* . . . and the rest follows easily. I prefer to wait. I prefer to buy this later. I prefer to think about this. We are our own best salespeople! *Sell yourself on your new priorities.*

SEE NO EVIL

Try this. During a tight month, don't put yourself in tempting situations. It's similar to establishing good eating habits.

Don't buy junk food. Don't go to the grocery store when you're hungry—you *can't help* but buy all kinds of food. If you don't want to spend money, don't go to shopping malls, factory outlets, and discount stores. What's the point? You will always find something to buy. Why do it this month when you can go next month instead? A month is really not so long to wait. Again, use the declarations above to help you. Say to yourself, "Normally I'd enjoy a field trip to the local mall, but today *I prefer* to take a bike ride instead and keep my Spending Plan on track. Maybe I'll ride by the mall . . . then again . . . *maybe not.*"

Bella thinks this is an excellent chapter, especially the part about being nice to salespeople and thanking them. While this comes quite naturally to her, she thinks more people need to remember it on their shopping sprees. Bella would like to clarify, however, that the above tactics are unnecessary at the cosmetics counter of a fine department store. She'd like to remind all our women readers that quality cosmetics last a long time and enhance your life every minute you wear them. Why, you might say they enhance the *world* by making it a more beautiful place. Anyone who would like Bella's personal attention can find her at . . .

Whoa, Bella! Our readers aren't looking for a cosmetics advertisement here.

Bella was just trying to be helpful.

SUMMARY

Emphasize your new goals over your former spending habits. Each spending opportunity is also an opportunity to remind yourself what is now important to you, and how you will benefit from your new goals. Do this frequently when you first start the *Money Without Madness System* because you'll be in an adjustment period. Realize that *eventually* you can buy *every-*

thing you want if you work it into your Spending Plan and stay with your plan each month.

TAKE ACTION

- Write down three comfortable responses to decline a spending opportunity. Practice saying them aloud to yourself.

- Decline the next five spending opportunities that salespeople present to you. Later, if you want to purchase the item, go back, say you changed your mind, and buy it.

- Go to a tempting store and practice using declarations to tell yourself what your new priorities are. Leave your wallet at home to guarantee success.

- Catch yourself whenever you say, "I can't afford it" or "I don't have the money." Rephrase your sentence right on the spot, starting with, "What I really mean is, I prefer . . ."

~ Chapter Twenty-Four
A Positive Attitude Will Help You Put Your Plan into Action

Growth is moving from one set of problems to a better set of problems.

—Successful uncle of a young businesswoman

No credit card payments, a pile of saved money, and a new money attitude—what do these have in common? All three enhance your life by reducing your money stress. Two of these cost you present day dollars; there's no way around it. The other is free. You may need patience to achieve complete **Credit Card Freedom** and work up to a consistent **Saving Habit,** but you can start changing your money attitude right now, no matter what your money situation is. It doesn't cost you one single U.S. greenback buck.

LESS STRESS

You will be stressed about money if you don't *know* what you need to know. You will also be stressed if you *know,* but you don't take action. Combining knowledge with a positive attitude launches you into action. The complete antidote for money stress is:

Knowledge + New Attitude = Action

Action = No Debt + Saved Money

No Debt + Saved Money = No Stress!

Who needs stress when the remedy is so easy? Already you are gaining the first ingredient, knowledge, by *learning* the steps outlined in this book. Your progress will be faster and easier if you take time to examine your attitudes about money and change any that are responsible for stress.

WORDS MATTER

The key to understanding your attitude is to notice the words you use. The key to changing your attitude is to change the words you use. Let's look at some general statements that pop up around the topic of money. Have you slipped into a few bad habits, occasionally using negative words and statements to describe the money in your life? Do any of the following sound like something you'd say?

- *I'll never get ahead!*
- *Money is always a problem.*
- *I never seem to have enough.*
- *What raise? Between taxes and bills there's nothing left!*
- *My paycheck is spent before I get it.*
- *I just got ahead and now this!*

First of all, join the club. Most of us have felt this way sometime in our lives. It works well to depress you. You can even get sympathy from others by using these comments. It's not hard to find folks who'll chime the money misery bell with you, and isn't it better to have others join in so you don't feel alone and different?

The problem is, these complaints don't help the situation. As a matter of fact, they do the opposite. They perpetuate a belief that your personal world consists of scarcity, sacrifice, and compromise, and it's beyond your control to change it.

DON'T BUY IT!

Make every word you say and every thought you think about your money a positive one. A new attitude is the key to new results. You change your underlying attitudes and beliefs by changing your thoughts and words. It will seem strange at first, unnatural perhaps, to shift. Continue. You need to loosen those old beliefs and let them wash away, replacing them with new truth.

Let's revise those comments:

- *I'll never get ahead!* becomes
  I'm making progress with my money every month and it's easy!

- *Money is always a problem* becomes
  Money is not *the problem.*

- *I never seem to have enough* becomes
  I always have enough for what I really *need and want.*

- *What raise? Between taxes and bills there's nothing left!* becomes
  I'll really enjoy the extra money from my raise.

- *My paycheck is spent before I get it* becomes
  I know exactly where I'll be spending this paycheck because I've already planned *it.*

- *I just got ahead, and now this!* becomes
  Thankfully, I just got ahead and can easily handle this.

AFFIRM YOUR COMMITMENT

Some people find it helpful to say positive statements (affirmations) to themselves in any area needing a jump start from negative to positive thinking. Affirmations are vehicles that take you from one place (negative attitudes) to another (positive beliefs). Repeat any of the following statements to yourself over and over each day until the positive attitudes become natural to you:

- *I always have everything in life I really want.*
- *I am prosperous and healthy.*
- *I like money and money likes me.*
- *Managing my money is fun and enjoyable.*
- *I see new progress in my finances every day.*

After using these prosperity affirmations for a while, they may bore you. Great progress! They've absorbed into your thought system and are no longer new. Customize more affirmations by listening for any doubts that surface while using these positive words. Create a variety of affirmations and take aim at any scarcity beliefs still lingering. Over time, you will achieve a positive attitude that will maintain itself with only occasional reminders.

LIKE YOUR MONEY

To attract money into your life you need to like money. The practical knowledge you're learning here works best to attract financial prosperity when your total attitude toward money is positive. Following the *Money Without Madness System* gives you an opportunity to feel good about your money, to give it attention and organization. You will feel positive as your money becomes easy to manage and responds to your directions. Your Spending Plan gives you the opportunity to understand your situation, know what to do about it, then make a plan and carry it out.

TO GUILT OR NOT TO GUILT ?

Should you feel guilty about liking money? NO! Not if you like money the way you like the other material things in your life: the Sierra mountain range in the distance; a new Lexus in the driveway; a favorite color (purple heather); a big house with an ocean view; black cats with yellow eyes. And money. What gets you into trouble is giving these things the wrong priority. You ask for Big Time Trouble when your priorities don't work, you ignore the signs that you are not happy, and you resist making changes.

Here's an example of the priority I give two things I like: Relationships come before money. Simple. If it costs money to be with a friend (which it sometimes does), I'll spend it. It works for me. Another one: Growth before money. I don't mind spending money to take a course or seminar if I can learn something valuable that will improve my life.

Prioritization of values is personal. If you have guilt about liking money, think about your priorities. What are your values? Where does money fit in? What is more important to you than money? Is money in the right place among your values?

IF YOU DON'T WANT MORE DOLLARS

Perhaps you aren't interested in using any extra energy to attract more money into your life. You're comfortable with your income and you have more important priorities. Great. There are many more important things in life. You will still benefit from keeping a positive attitude toward the money you have. Following the *Money Without Madness System* brings simplicity to your life and saves you time. It frees you to focus on the other more important areas of your life.

GOOD OR GREED?

Letting money go is good, clutching money is greed. You let money go when you spend it, pay your bills, and give it away. Even when you put it into savings you let it go because your savings are loaned to others to help their dreams come true. You let go of money when you invest. Your dollars are a vote of confidence in the purpose of the investment and the people running it. Whenever you let your money circulate in positive ways, you get a return. Sometimes you get a monetary return as you expected (from investments), sometimes a material return (when you buy something), sometimes a feeling (when you donate).

Unless you stash your cash in a sack, you circulate money. So what is greed? Greed is focusing your money only on your own gains. It is an attitude more than an action. When I was in my twenties, I spent money on investments I didn't understand or believe in purely to make money. Instead of gaining, I acquired an anti-Midas touch and the only return I got was some wise words from my father, "Bears and bulls make money—hogs go broke." Later, I made my investment choices with fewer dollars and a bigger attitude. Today, I find the gains bring me growth and the losses bring me laughs.

Bella thinks this might be her favorite chapter. No more grumbling about money from her! She's going to start liking her money, taking care of it, and enjoying it right away.

SUMMARY

Make positive statements about your money and your prosperity will grow. Whatever you value in life, you will have. Hold a friendly attitude toward money and welcome it into your life. Be willing to hold money lightly and happily, not to clutch it or clutch for it. Recognize that money's role is merely to bring good things to you; it is not an end in itself. Money is only as powerful as what you do with it. Let it do what you want it to do in your life.

TAKE ACTION:

- Think about what prosperity is for you. Create five affirmations that ring true.

- Say to yourself *I am prosperous* one hundred times a day for seven days in a row. Say it like it's true. Notice any changes?

- Write down five things you value more than money—your time, convenience, health, beauty, security. OK, that was too easy—think of five more. Freedom, family . . .

Chapter Twenty-Five

From Anxiety to Excitement

> *If you think you can, you're right.*
>
> *If you think you can't, you're right.*
>
> —Cosmetics salesperson in a fine
> department store

Are you ready to improve an important part of your life, to make a change for the better? Do you believe you can do it? What should you expect as you begin to add new habits to your life and change old ones? Any of the following:

AFTER FINISHING THE BOOK

Excitement!

You always wanted the benefits and freedom of managing your money. You never knew it could be so easy.

What to Do About It

Enjoy it. Use the energy to jump start your new program. Accomplish all your ACTION ITEMS immediately. Make your way through *The Twelve Steps to Financial Freedom.*

Apprehension

You're not sure you can really do all the steps. It looks sort of complicated. Especially the part about the bank statement.

What to Do About It

Break the steps down into simpler tasks. Instead of trying to do all the steps in your Money Mechanics this month, pick the one you like best and start with that. What is it? Doing next month's Spending Plan? Paying all your bills at once? Leave checkbook balancing until later if it overwhelms you. Pick one step from *The Twelve Steps to Financial Freedom* that you believe you can do right now, and do it. Reread parts of this book whenever you are ready to take on another step so the information is fresh.

Think of the most important benefit you will gain from improving your money management skills. Further prosperity? Financial confidence? Freedom from money worries? Keep your number-one benefit clearly in mind so you always know why you want to move forward. If the work overwhelms you, start with some of the positive word techniques we talked about in the last chapter. Create some affirmations and use them.

Resistance

All this looks like a good idea, but you'd rather wait to start changing your life. You have a sneaky feeling if you look too closely at your money you'll feel guilty. The guilt might stay with you until you change your spending behavior and you're not ready to do that. You know you can always do this later anyway, so why start now?

What to Do about It

Make a deal with yourself: Do the Money Mechanics every month, simply as an experiment. Develop just that one habit. Your only response to the information is, "Oh, that's interesting." Don't make changes you don't want to make in your spending. Give yourself plenty of time for this step—years if necessary. Don't even think about taking on *The Twelve Steps to Financial Freedom* until you want to. When you're ready, you'll have the tools you need to make immediate gains.

BEGINNING YOUR MONEY MECHANICS

Satisfaction

It feels good to finally tackle this area, which has been a mystery for so long. Once you start, it's easy to get yourself organized. Soon your Money Mechanics becomes second nature to you.

What to Do about It

Relax into your new habits. Continue your progress on *The Twelve Steps to Financial Freedom*. Work at a steady, satisfying pace. Don't become overly aggressive in achieving them.

Frustration

You begin with the best of intentions but can't remain positive. Your Money Mechanics starts looking too much like work, not fun at all. The rest of *The Twelve Steps to Financial Freedom* seems impossible to accomplish—in this lifetime!

What to Do about It

Slow down. Start by doing one step at a time each month. As that works and becomes a habit, add another step. For instance, simply pay all your bills at one time. Later, add the checkbook balancing step. Then add the Spending Plan for next month. When you build up in small stages, you won't be so overwhelmed.

Loss of Interest

The Twelve Steps to Financial Freedom become boring and doing your Money Mechanics feels like a chore. It doesn't appear to add anything to your life, and you really don't see how you'll ever get ahead. Why bother?

What to Do about It

Postpone making decisions when you're emotionally down. Loss of interest or ambivalence hides an underlying belief that you can't get what you really want—so you don't want to want it. When negative feelings strike, attend to your mood first. Get some rest, relaxation, mild exercise, and healthful food. Review your goals again when you are in a more positive, or at least neutral, frame of mind. Think about what benefits you want from the money in your life. Create some affirmations for those benefits and use them frequently. Read one of the prosperity books listed in Appendix A at the end of this book.

Continue doing just your Money Mechanics every month regardless of the rest of your financial situation. Managing your money gives you a sense of control over part of your world. Put *The Twelve Steps to Financial Freedom* on hold until you are ready. Give yourself time—several months, perhaps—to convert your ambivalence into more positive beliefs.

AFTER DOING YOUR MONEY MECHANICS

Enjoyment

You look forward to seeing your progress at the end of the month and planning next month's spending.

Confidence

You know exactly what you can buy now and how new purchases will affect your total financial situation. You make financial decisions with full information and no apprehension. You know how to control your outflows and you are reaching your goals.

Peace

Having control over your money brings you a sense of peace. You're not afraid of unknowns. You know exactly how much money you need for the material things you want in life. You live comfortably with what you have now and can gain greater prosperity if you choose to.

What to Do about It

Congratulate yourself! You are ready to move to the next stage of your financial goals whenever you want.

TIME IS ON YOUR SIDE

Give yourself plenty of time to work through **The Twelve Steps to Financial Freedom,** and make the three key money habits part of your life. You may need as many as five years to work through them. This is realistic. There is a natural rhythm to bringing these changes into your life. Moving too fast causes burn-out, disappointment, and discouragement. If you feel this coming on, put your progress on hold. Slow down. Take a small backslide to avoid a major one. Instead of focusing on how long it will take you to pay off your credit card debt or start a *Saving Habit,* focus only on each month's progress. If it doesn't come easily, lower your monthly expectations until it does. Time passes faster when you're enjoying your life. Your goals will be accomplished soon enough. Learn to move slowly and know your plan is working.

Bella says, "Arrivederci." She's enjoyed being with you. With a good-bye wave, our heroine mounts her white Honda scooter and speeds off into the sunset—her long, *natural* strawberry blonde hair flowing behind her. She's off to complete her TAKE ACTION and move forward on *The Twelve Steps to Financial Freedom.* She'll see you again in the land of Money Mechanics!

Thank you, Bella. We appreciate everything you've shared with us. Couldn't have done it without you. Have fun in Cancun!

SUMMARY

Start now! Anyone can use Spending Plans and Money Mechanics to accomplish *The Twelve Steps to Financial Freedom.* Whether you choose to or not is up to you. It will take desire, patience, and consistency to add these improvements to your life. Do it gradually. Five years from now you'll be five years older. Think about what you want your life to look like then. Wouldn't you rather gain a sense of enjoyment, confidence, and peace with your finances than still be living with monetary chaos and uncertainty? If you want financial prosperity in your life, you need to know how to handle it. Sooner or later you'll need these skills. Get started now and you'll get there sooner. Don't ever say "I can't . . ." about anything. You *can* do whatever you *want* to do. If you want greater prosperity, you will have it.

TAKE ACTION

- Calculate an approximate timetable to complete *The Twelve Steps to Financial Freedom*. Add a year. Yes, a year.

- Have fun with your money!

Endings and Beginnings

If it don't work small,
It won't work big.

—Businessman, on growing a company

You won't get more of something unless you take care of what you have. If you want more money, learn how to take care of the money you have. If you want more time, give it to yourself by using your Money Mechanics to streamline your money chores. Peace of mind? Take charge of your money and head toward your goals. Then breathe easy knowing you're taking action.

The *Money Without Madness System* gives you freedom and paves the way for more prosperity in your life. In any economic climate, from high-growth to high-uncertainty, you'll get more from your money when you know how to manage it. Use the *Money Without Madness System* until it becomes second nature to you. Then continue. Make it like driving the car that is so familiar it seems to be part of you. The *Money Without Madness System* is like that car—it drives you to your financial goals.

Put your new knowledge into action *now* and watch the results roll in!

Appendix A

Further Reading

Prosperity Books

Bolle, Richard. *What Color is Your Parachute?* Berkeley, CA: Ten Speed Press, 1992.

Dyer, Wayne. *You'll See It When You Believe It.* New York: Avon Books, 1989.

Gawain, Shakti. *Creative Visualization.* New York: Bantam Books, 1983.

Hill, Napoleon. *Think and Grow Rich.* New York: Fawcett Crest, 1987.

Peale, Norman Vincent. *The Power of Positive Thinking.* New York: Fawcett Crest, 1987.

Ponder, Catherine. *Open Your Mind to Receive.* Marina del Rey, CA: DeVorss & Company, 1983. (*Note:* Catherine Ponder has written over a dozen books on prosperity including *The Dynamic Laws of Prosperity, The Secret of Unlimited Prosperity,* and *Dare to Prosper!)*

Money Management Books

Cooke, Robert A. *Personal Finance for Busy People.* New York: McGraw Hill, 1998.

Orman, Suze. *The 9 Steps to Financial Freedom: Practical and Spiritual Steps So You Can Stop Worrying.* New York: Random House, 1997.

Ortalda, Robert A., Jr. *How to Live Within Your Means and Still Finance Your Dreams.* New York: Fireside, 1990.

Help for High Debt

Bryon, Mark and Julia Cameron. *The Money Drunk: 90 Days to Financial Freedom.* New York: Ballantine Books, 1992.

Mundis, Jerold. *How to Get Out of Debt, Stay Out of Debt, and Live Prosperously:Based on the Proven Principles and Techniques of Debtors Anonymous.* New York, Bantam Books, 1990.

Debtors Anonymous
General Service Board
PO Box 888
Needham, MA 02492-0009
Phone (781) 453-2743

Forms & Resources

These forms will help you with your Money Mechanics and with your progress on *The Twelve Steps to Financial Freedom*.

Spending Plan

Use these for your Master Spending Plan and your Actual Spending Plans. Make as many copies as you like. Keep one as a blank to copy.

The Twelve Steps to Financial Freedom

This is the list to help you develop the three key money habits:

1. *Manage Your Money Monthly.*

2. *Gain Credit Card Freedom.*

3. *Start Saving Now.*

SPENDING PLAN

Month/Yr _____ *End Date* _____ *No./Weeks* _____

INCOME		Plan	Actual	Diff.
	Date	Amount		
Net Pay	_____	_____		
Other	_____	_____	_____	_____
	_____	_____	_____	_____
Bottom Line —Last Month Surplus		_____	_____	
TOTAL INCOME		☐	☐	☐

EXPENSES	Plan	Actual	Diff.
Bottom Line-Last Month Negative	☐	☐	
Checks			
_____	_____	_____	
_____	_____	_____	
_____	_____	_____	
_____	_____	_____	
_____	_____	_____	
_____	_____	_____	
_____	_____	_____	
_____	_____	_____	
_____	_____	_____	
Total Checks	☐	☐	☐
Cash $_____ x _____	☐	☐	☐
dollars weeks			
Flexible Money _____	_____	_____	
_____	_____	_____	
Total Flexible Money	☐	☐	☐
Credit Card Freedom			
_____	_____	_____	
_____	_____	_____	
_____	_____	_____	
Total Credit Card Freedom	☐	☐	☐
Start Saving Now! YES!	☐	☐	☐
TOTAL EXPENSES	☐	☐	☐

BOTTOM LINE	Plan	Actual	Diff.
(Income minus expenses)	☐	☐	☐

THE TWELVE STEPS TO FINANCIAL FREEDOM

❏ 1. Get an income.

❏ 2. Complete your first monthly Spending Plan.

❏ 3. Do your Money Mechanics every month.

❏ 4. Close *all* your department store charge accounts to future charges.

   (Do your Money Mechanics every month!)

❏ 5. Stop charging on *all* other credit cards except to make emergency payments and occasional convenience purchases.

❏ 6. Make at least the *minimum* payments on all credit card debt (more if you can).

   (Do your Money Mechanics every month!)

❏ 7. *Follow* your Spending Plan.

❏ 8. Save 5% of your take-home income every month.

❏ 9. Pay off *all* credit card debt. Close all but two major credit cards.

   (Do your Money Mechanics every month!)

❏ 10. Save 7% of your take-home income every month.

❏ 11. Save 10% of your take-home income every month.

   (Do your Money Mechanics every month!)

❏ 12. Indulge yourself in something you really want. You deserve it!

Conceptual Index

ATTITUDE

- Start changing your money attitude now. 179

- The key to changing your attitude is to change the words you use. 180

- Make every word you say and every thought you think about your money a positive one. 181

BETTER BASICS

- It's natural to seek quiet retreat and simplify our lifestyles. 163

- Your biggest money savers—creativity and an open mind. 166

- Don't give up anything—think about how to do it differently and *enjoy* doing it differently. 166

- If the choice isn't self-motivated, you won't be content and the changes won't last. 167

BILLS

- Do it Fast, Do it Right, Do it Once. 104

- Get an address stamp or labels. They are cheap and save you time. 106

- Use the last bill you receive every month to remind yourself to start your Money Mechanics. 117

BREAKS

- Self-designated breaks are fine, but interruptions cause errors that frustrate you. 91

BUDGETS

- Traditional budgets don't work. 3

CASH CUSHION

- Make building a Cash Cushion your first savings goal. 119

- Your Cash Cushion never leaves, it is just used and replenished. 117

- You're not going to spend your Cash Cushion so don't include it in your Spending Plan. 119

- A Cash Cushion is a necessity when you don't get paid at regular intervals. 131

CASH TO BURN

- Repetitive expenses and small purchases are covered with a constant amount of weekly cash. 12

- Smooth your spending into a constant amount each week and spend it freely on whatever you want. 24

- Cash to Burn covers your basic spending needs—it pays for your well-being. 26

- Look in your wallet and if you don't like what you don't see, remember it is only a matter of a few days until it will be full again. 25

CHECKBOOK BALANCING

- The purpose of balancing your checkbook is to find differences between the total you show and the total the bank shows on its statement. 93

- Any amounts in your checkbook and not on the bank's statement are called outstanding items. 94

- Balance your bank statement soon after it arrives and you will have fewer outstanding items causing differences. 95

- Use a calculator and do it twice. 95

CONFIDENCE

- Learning to organize your money at the basic level gives you the confidence you need for higher levels of financial management. 90

COUPLES

- The Household account covers shared expenses. 147

- The Spending Plan is a useful discussion tool for shared money and goals. 148

- The Money Manager needs to be free of judgment toward spending styles different from his or her own. 150

- The purpose of managing the shared money is to control the money, not the partner. 150

- Switching roles is a good idea. Then both partners will be able to handle the money if they ever need to. 150

CREDIT CARDS

- Credit cards provide purchasing and payment convenience, and credit for emergencies. 48

- Credit cards are a source of help in small doses, a loss of freedom in large doses. 48

- The difference between having a credit card that *helps* you and a credit card that *hurts* you is *how you use it.* 48

- Credit cards are great shifters of payments from the current month to the next. 48

- Think of your available credit as insurance; you pay a small annual fee to reduce your risk. 49

- When you pay for everyday purchases with current money, the past will not haunt you. When you pay with a credit card, the ghost of your past purchases visits frequently to rattle your bucks. 51

- Charging causes charging. 51

- As long as you pay your credit card balance in full, your cards are working for you. If not, you're working for your cards. 54

DEBT

- It is may be necessary to use debt to fund a house, car, and sometimes a college degree. It is not necessary to fund your lifestyle with credit card debt. 51

- Eliminate credit card debt forever! 51

EMERGENCIES

- You may not be able to control the emergency, but you can control the payment by using your credit card. 40

- It's better to take your time with an emergency payment, even at additional cost, than to add to your troubles by skimping on the rest of your money and therefore your well-being. 39–40

- When your credit cards are at their limits, you have nowhere to go for emergency money. 51

FILING

- Keep your shoebox free of everything but financial paperwork. 109

FINANCIAL FALLACIES

- It's tempting to convince yourself there really won't be any surprises each month so your Flexible Money can be lower. 67

- Don't get so carried away you deny yourself enough Flexible Money. 67

- Don't go too skinny on your Cash to Burn. 68

FLEXIBLE MONEY

- Many Spending Plans fail, both in personal lives and business enterprises, because little or no provision is made for unknowns. 37

- Your Flexible Money covers emergencies, desires, and spontaneous spending. 38

- Plan the purchase or plan the payment. 38

- Use checks to pay for your Flexible Money purchases. 40

- Start with 10% and adjust it up or down after you've worked with it for a while. 44

- The more activity, possessions, and people in your life, the more you will have spending surprises. 44

GIVING

- Make sure you are externally focused instead of self-focused. 142

- Expect your highest return to be how you feel about yourself instead of a bigger bank account. Do not confuse donating with investing. 142

- If you give large amounts to one organization, make monthly payments instead of weekly ones. 143

GOALS

- Living these habits is a prerequisite for success with future goals. 156

- Make easy, gradual changes so you know they are real rather than temporary changes sparked by fleeting motivation. 157

- Money responds beautifully to constant and focused attention over a period of time. 90

GREED

- Greed is an attitude more than an action. 184

- Greed is focusing your money only on your own gains. 184

GUILT

- If you have guilt about liking money, think about your priorities. Is money in the right place among your values? 183

MONEY'S ESCAPE ROUTES

- There are only three ways your hard-earned funds can leave you: cash, check, and charge. 11

MONEY MECHANICS

- Money Mechanics is the activity of managing your money toward your goals. 87

- Create new ideas and put them to work. 89

MOTIVATION

- Break the steps down into simpler tasks. 188

- Pick one step from *The Twelve Steps to Financial Freedom* that you believe you can do right now, and do it. 188

- Reread parts of this book to give you a fresh start. 188

- Keep your number-one benefit clearly in mind so you know why you want to move forward. 188

- If the work overwhelms you, start with some affirmations. 188

- Make a deal with yourself: Do the Money Mechanics only. 189

- Slow down. Do one step well before adding another. 190

- Postpone making decisions when you're ambivalent. Use affirmations to improve your mood. 190

- Give yourself plenty of time. Learn to move slowly and know your plan is working. 190

- Focus on each month's progress. 192

ORGANIZATION

- Money likes to be organized. 90

REWARDS

- Reward yourself as you progress through your goals. 158

- Make sure the reward is consistent with your new money goals. 158

- Give meaning to something ordinary to symbolize your financial achievement. 158

ROUNDING

- Rounding simplifies the numbers you are working with, gives you fewer digits to record, and makes significant numbers easier to remember. 123

SAVINGS

- Saving money is the equivalent of making a profit in a healthy business. 56

- Do not mix your saved money with your checking account money. 59

- One of the best times to start saving, or to move to a higher savings percentage, is when you receive a raise. 59

- With a steady amount of money always building your savings, you are free to spend it, invest it, and use it for any of your financial goals. 56

SPENDING PLAN

- Your Master Spending Plan gives you the overview of your financial picture, and your Actual Spending Plan goes into the details of each month's cash flow. 4

- Your Actual Spending Plan is the tool that turns theory and ideas into reality. 75

- Now you strategize, play with the numbers, manipulate your money on paper, and see what options you have. 75

SPONTANEOUS SPENDING

- Leave some money unidentified in your Flexible Money category for truly spontaneous spending. 40

STRESS

- You will be stressed about money if you don't know what you need to know, and also if you know but don't take action. 179

SUCCESS

- Success with money requires knowledge, direction, and action. 87

- Visualize your Spending Plan coming in on target and manage your spending so it happens. 90

TAXES

- Plan for a refund. 135

- Claiming zero withholding allowances tells your employer to take out more taxes than claiming five. 135

- You owe the same amount of tax whether or not it is deducted throughout the year. 137

- Lower your tax expense by using all the loopholes available to you as prescribed by your tax preparer. 137

- A good time to lower your W-4 allowances is when you get a raise. 137

THANK YOU ANYWAY

- Count on going through an adjustment period as your spending behavior shifts from unplanned to planned spending. 170

- Use spending opportunities to remind yourself what your new choices and priorities are, and to demonstrate your new spending behavior. 169

- Guard against statements convincing yourself expensive merchandise is frivolous. Later, when you have abundant funds you may deny yourself the pleasure of high quality items. 172

- In tempting spending situations, think about your financial goals. 174

- Remember to thank the salesperson. 174

- During a tight month, don't put yourself in tempting situations. 175

TIMING

- To do your Money Mechanics you need your bills and your bank statement together at one time. 113

- Major bank credit cards are often flexible with their billing cycles. 114

- Do not jeopardize a good credit history for the sake of convenience, because you can have both. 115

TIPS

- Accumulate cash tips one week and use them for next week's Cash to Burn. 131

UNPREDICTABLE INCOME

- The Ebb and Flow method allows your level of spending to fluctuate up and down with changes in your income. 127–128

- The Steady State method gives you a constant level of spending regardless of the ups and downs of your income. 130

WANT LIST

- When your wanting goes beyond the Flexible Money available to you this month, start a Want List. 38

- As money becomes available it is destined to be spent on meaningful purchases rather than to disappear quickly on impulse buys. 39

WORDS

- Don't say you "can't afford" something, or you "don't have the money," unless you *want* it to be true. 172

- Start with the words, *I prefer* . . . and the rest follows easily. 175

WORRY

- If you find yourself worrying throughout the month, remember your commitment to following your Spending Plan and improve your situation. 82

Index

The buck stops here.

—President Harry S. Truman

About the Author

Karen Brigham, CPA, is a financial consultant living in Mountain View, California. She has a BS in Accounting from the University of Denver and an MBA from Santa Clara University, and she has held financial management positions with several successful start-up companies in Silicon Valley. She enjoys ballroom, swing, and Latin dancing, hiking the Santa Cruz mountains, and desert camping. Her goal is to help nonfinancial people at all income levels enjoy their money.

The author invites you to visit the web site at www.moneywithoutmadness.com. You may email her at karen@moneywithoutmadness.com, or write her at PO Box 390807, Mountain View, CA 94039-0807.